Nancy Lam
Stirs it up

DEDICATION

To my husband and my three girls, my sister Amy in Singapore, Peggy Poon, Eddy and Anne Lim, and Lily Lane – and to all my customers and friends who have stood by me when times were hard, especially Marc and Susanna Hendriks.

SERVING QUANTITIES

All the recipes in this book have been planned on the basis that each will form part of a typical Southeast Asian meal, where 4 people will share 4 or 5 different dishes, plus rice or noodles. If you are planning to cook for fewer people, you are best advised to make fewer dishes (minimum 3), rather than scale down the ingredients in any of the dishes. Suggestions on how to combine these recipes into satisfying and balanced meals are given on pages 148-154.

Throughout the book both metric and imperial quantities are given. Use either all metric or all imperial, as the two are not necessarily interchangeable.

Editor & Project Manager: Lewis Esson
Design: Nigel Soper
Colour Photography: John Lawrence Jones
Black-and-white Photography: John Millar
Food for Photography: Nancy Lam and Linda McLean
Hair Styling and Make-up: Yangtze Lam-Nyatedzu

First published in 1997 by Fourth Estate Ltd, 6 Salem Road, London W2 4BU

This edition produced for
The Book People Ltd,
Hall Wood Avenue,
Haydock, St.Helens
WA11 9UL

ISBN 1-85702-796-5

Colour separations by Rapida Group plc, London
Printed and bound in Italy by L.E.G.O., Vicenza

Nancy Lam

Nancy Lam Stirs It Up

> Enak! Enak! The chillies are coming to get you!

TED SMART

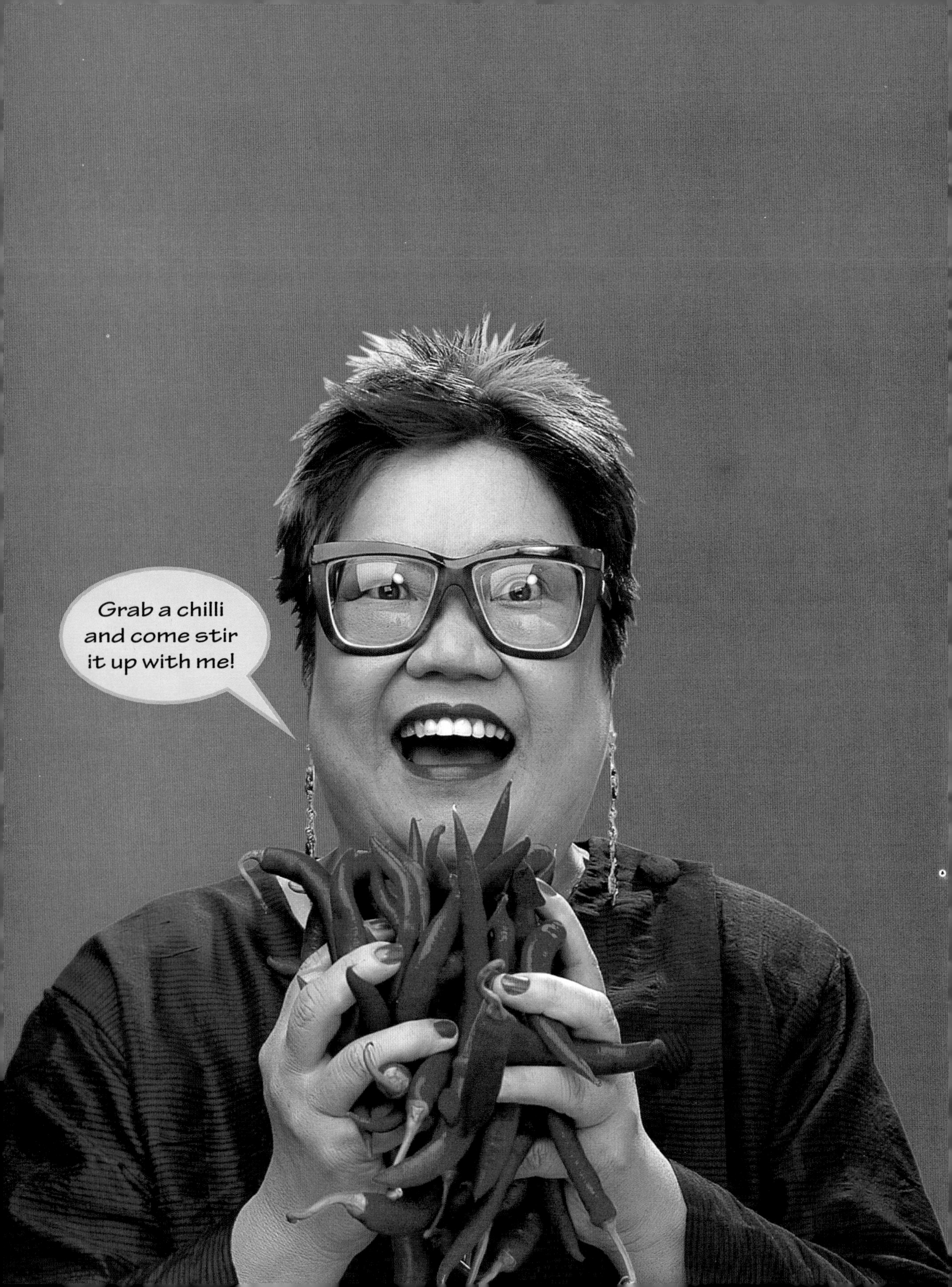
Grab a chilli and come stir it up with me!

Contents

The World of Nancy Lam

Enak Enak (Yum Yum). What made this small restaurant in Lavender Hill one of South London's worst-kept secrets? What made Nancy Lam and Ben among the most popular hosts in the country and the darlings of Channel 5? Read on and you may get some idea...

This is my world and you're welcome to it!

Q. What are the influences on the way you cook?

A. My background, tradition and upbringing all came to me from my Indonesian grandmother. She taught me that food should be cooked with love and inspiration.

Q. Why do you cook what you cook?

A. I cook traditional dishes that are appetizing, simple to cook, easy to recognize, easy to eat – and I don't go in for lots of decoration!

Q. Why did you open the restaurant?

A. To make a living and as a challenge – I also wanted to cook and to be able to choose the dishes that were to be served.

You also get to do the washing up!

Q. Are there any funny stories about getting it up and running?

A. A couple came in very late one night just after we had opened and sat down like schoolkids about to get detention, as we had been a bit reluctant to serve them at 11 p.m. They were so scared they both ordered the same *rendang* and boiled rice as they obviously wanted to get out as soon as possible. I went over and suggested they change their order as it would be impractical. When the lady got up to go to the loo I told her gently that they should relax and enjoy the food. To my surprise they were back next day... nice and early. Today they are great friends. I even convinced them to discard their pills and get cooking themselves and now they have a lovely baby boy.

There must be an easier way to earn a living!

The lady of another couple who came into the restaurant in those early days began sobbing, so I assumed her man had been giving her trouble. I went over and told him off in front of all the other customers, so I thought we'd never see them again. The next day they were back and all was smiles... now they too are great friends – and actually got married in the restaurant.

Oh no! Not another earthquake!

A lady having dinner told me that she had discovered that her only son was gay and shed tears like Niobe. I already knew because her son and his boyfriend came regularly to the restaurant and had become good friends. After a long discussion, I said to Mum, 'Do you want to lose a son?' She said 'No', and we are all now good friends.

Q. Who were the oddest customers you ever had?

A. I once had a lady who had ordered Nasi Goreng tell me that she was having an orgasm under the table.

One young girl at the end of her meals would always offer to show her (rather lovely) tits for a brandy... it was amazing how many punters were only too willing to send her over a nightcap!

Nancy's Pantry

● ● ● ● ● ● ● ● ● ●

People worry about having to find lots of unusual ingredients when cooking food like mine. However, just a slight expansion of the basic items you keep stocked in your larder, fridge, freezer and store-cupboard will put you in a position to have a go at my recipes whenever you feel so inclined.

It is also amazing how many unexpected situations you can then take in your stride if your kitchen is well stocked. Obviously you don't need to have all of the following all of the time, but you'll find that stocking some of these items will allow you to enrich your normal everyday cooking, whether or not you're cooking Southeast Asian food – so none of it will go to waste and it will also help you ring more changes in family meals, as well as allow you to entertain effortlessly.

As the store-cupboard is the area in which most investment is required, I've divided my list of recommendations for that into a 'basic' section (listing items that really are necessary, but which will always come in handy for any type of cooking) and a 'more adventurous' add-on for those really wanting to get down to some serious stirring.

● ● ● ● ● ● ● ● ● ●

In the larder:
half-dozen eggs
2 or 3 heads of garlic
packet of sea salt
packet of black peppercorns
4 or 5 onions
3 or 4 red onions
packet of shallots
4 or 5 lemons
3 or 4 limes
small bag of potatoes

On the window-sill:
small pots of fresh herbs, especially
coriander
basil

In the fridge:
packet of ready-washed salad leaves
large bunch of spring onions
500 g / 1 lb tomatoes
large head of pak-choi
2–3 red/yellow/orange peppers
handful of chilli peppers
bunch of lemon grass stalks
large piece of ginger root
large piece of galangal root
large piece of turmeric root

In the freezer:
225 g / 8 oz leaf spinach
115 g/ 4 oz small garden peas
1.1 litre / 2 pints chicken stock
packet of frozen tiger prawns
packet of won ton wrappers

In the store-cupboard:
BASIC
450 g / 1 lb American long-grain or Thai fragrant rice
450 g / 1 lb Oriental noodles
packet of cornflour
bottle of sunflower oil
small bottle of chilli oil
small bottle of dark sesame oil
bottle of good-quality soy sauce
bottle of Worcestershire sauce
bottle of chilli sauce
bottle of fish sauce
bottle of oyster sauce *(keep in the fridge once opened)*
whole cloves
cinnamon sticks
ground cinnamon
fennel seeds
cardamom pods
cumin seeds
dried chillies
chilli powder
sesame seeds
ground turmeric
garlic powder
ground coriander
ground fenugreek
poppy seeds
curry powder
five-spice powder
soft brown sugar
clear honey and/or maple syrup
walnut halves
cashew nuts

dry-roasted peanuts
packet of desiccated coconut
bottle of dry white wine
small bottle of brandy
wooden satay sticks *(10–15 cm / 4–6 inches long)*

MORE ADVENTUROUS
bottle of blachan *(keep it tightly closed as it has a powerful smell)*
block of tamarind pulp
dried lime leaves
dried Chinese mushrooms
candlenuts
bottle of rice wine or dry sherry
bottle of rice vinegar
bottle of hoisin sauce *(keep in the fridge once opened)*
bottle of black bean sauce *(keep in the fridge once opened)*
bottle of yellow bean sauce *(keep in the fridge once opened)*
coconut powder
ketjap manis

In cans:
water chestnuts
crab meat
coconut milk
sweetcorn kernels

Nancy's Pots and Pans

You don't really need any fancy equipment to cook my sort of food – you can do most things with ordinary everyday kit. However, the following might come in handy:

Wok

These are invaluable for stir-frying, as the shape and the thin light metal help get heat into the food as quickly as possible. The shape also allows you to push food that is more or less cooked up the sides, while new additions are stirred down in the bottom of the pan.

Nevertheless you can stir-fry quite readily in a good big deep frying pan. Don't go buying expensive woks from big manufacturers, the bog-standard ones you see in Chinese supermarkets are ideal. They may not last all that long, but they are so cheap you can afford to replace them regularly.

One important note: if you are going to get seriously into Southeast Asian flavours and use a lot of tamarind, then it might be a good idea to invest in a stainless-steel or non-stick wok, as tamarind juice is very acid and reacts with the other metal surfaces – it isn't dangerous, but it will discolour the pans and perhaps give you more minerals (especially aluminium, for example) in your food than you would like!

Bamboo Steamer

As with woks, you really don't need expensive purpose-made metal steaming pans, the dirt-cheap tiered bamboo steamers you get in Chinese supermarkets are ideal for the purpose *(see page 52)*. You can use them in combination with any suitable saucepan and, of course, you can add tier upon tier – so you could do a whole steamed meal at one go!

Those little collapsible metal steaming platforms which fit inside ordinary saucepans are OK, but I find you can never get enough water under them to give you a good head of steam for long enough without worrying about topping up.

Griddle Pan

The nice seared crust of grilled food makes a good counterpoint to other types of food in a balanced meal, but it is sometimes difficult to get domestic grills hot enough to give you good results (and we know you can't use the barbecue most of the year in this country!). The answer is the griddle or grilling pan, which is made of cast iron and so takes up lots of heat from the hob to deliver a nice searing temperature on contact. The top is usually ridged to give you that attractive deep brown hatching you associate with barbecued food. These griddles, because their construction is so simple, are remarkably inexpensive and well worth the investment. See Ben's Guide to Good Grilling *(page 94)* for how to use them.

Pestle and Mortar

You will see that I like to grind a lot of ingredients, not just the obvious whole spices and nuts, but things like onions and lemon grass. Obviously, if you are busy – or lazy – you can do this in a food processor, but it is all too easy to over-work them to a mush when you do it this way. I therefore much prefer using a pestle *(ulek ulek)* and mortar – like the one illustrated, which has been in my family for over a century. Get a big sturdy one – you really need to bash it, so something dainty is useless!

Rice Cooker

These little electric slow cookers are not really necessary, but my God they do make a difference if you cook rice regularly, especially in large quantities – I don't know how I'd manage without mine in the restaurant. They cook very gently and switch themselves off automatically at just the right point, then keeping the rice nice and warm. They come in different sizes, so get a good big one as they don't have to be filled every time and it is for large quantities that they really come into their own.

Won ton hussy?

Soups and Starters

Soups can be fairly substantial items in my part of the world, eaten with rice as one-dish meals at lunch (or even breakfast). Any of the soup recipes given here will serve four as a first course or two as a one-dish meal. It is also very easy to increase the amount of soup by just making and using more chicken stock, so that you can have second helpings. Of course, the secret of a good tasty soup is a good rich, well-flavoured stock and for that you generally need nothing more than bones and long slow cooking – the longer you simmer them, the richer the resulting stock will be.

Halibut and Pineapple Soup

500 g / 1 lb skinned halibut fillets
1 medium pineapple
½ chilli, deseeded and coarsely chopped
2 medium onions
5-mm / ¼-inch piece of fresh turmeric *(see page 66)*, peeled
1 stalk of lemon grass *(see page 48)*
¼ teaspoon shrimp paste *(blachan, see right)*
¼ teaspoon salt
¼ teaspoon sugar
red chilli peppers, for garnish *(optional)*

PREPARATION

Rinse the fish fillets, pat them dry with paper towels and cut them into bite-sized cubes.
Peel the pineapple, making sure no 'eyes' are left, slice it thinly and remove the hard cores *(see page 142)*.
Using a pestle and mortar or food processor, grind the chilli, onions and turmeric to a paste.
Bash the lemon grass stalk with a mallet or the heel of a large knife.

COOKING

Put the lemon grass in a saucepan with 1 litre / 1¾ pints water and bring to the boil. Stir in the chilli and onion paste, together with the shrimp paste. Simmer for 30 minutes.
Add the pineapple slices and simmer for 15 minutes more. Add the fish, the salt and sugar, and simmer very gently for 5-7 minutes, until the fish is cooked through.
The soup may be served hot or allowed to cool and be served chilled. If you like, garnish it with red chilli peppers split lengthwise into flower shapes as shown.

Blachan

Also known as *balachan, balachong* or *trasi* in Indonesia, this is a flavouring preparation that is essential in much of the cooking of Southeast Asia. It is made from dried salted shrimp which have been allowed to ferment in the sun and then pounded to a paste, so it is pretty powerful stuff and only a little is usually needed in any dish. Some people are really quite alarmed by the strong smell, but that goes when it is cooked. It keeps well in the refrigerator, tightly wrapped or in a well-sealed jar as the aroma is really pervasive. If you can't get any, then anchovy essence or paste will give you a little of the effect, but the dish won't taste nearly as good.

Won Ton Soup

Prawn and Pork Dumplings in Chicken Stock

10 won ton wrappers *(see below)*

FOR THE FILLING:
275 g / 10 oz raw prawns, shelled and deveined *(see page 33)*
115 g / 4 oz minced lean pork
2 tablespoons soy sauce
2 teaspoons sesame oil
1 teaspoon cornflour
½ teaspoon freshly ground black pepper
275 g / 10 oz canned water chestnuts, drained and finely chopped
3 spring onions, chopped
1 egg, lightly beaten

FOR THE CHICKEN STOCK:
1 kg / 2 lb chicken bones

TO DRESS:
more sesame oil, fish sauce, more soy sauce

PREPARATION
First prepare the chicken stock. Put the chicken bones in a large pan and just cover with water. Bring to the boil and simmer for at least 2 hours (the longer you simmer them, the richer the stock). Prepare the filling for the won tons: in a blender or food processor, mince the prawns with the pork, soy sauce, sesame oil, cornflour and the pepper. Transfer to a bowl and stir in the water chestnuts, 2 of the chopped spring onions and the egg. Put 1 teaspoon of the filling mixture in the middle of each won ton wrapper. Lightly moisten the edges of the wrapper around the filling and gather up the edges like a pouch, then press the top firmly to seal.

COOKING
Bring a large pan of water to a good rolling boil. Drop in the filled won tons and bring the water back to the boil as quickly as possible. As soon as the won tons float to the top they are ready. Fish them out of the pan with a slotted spoon, draining well (this process gets rid of all the starch).
Place the won tons in another pan, pour in the hot stock (leaving the bones behind, of course) and simmer for 1 or 2 minutes more. Dish up into serving bowls and dress with more sesame oil, fish sauce and soy sauce to taste. Garnish with the remaining chopped spring onion.

Mei Mei Soup

60 g / 2 oz dried Chinese mushrooms
200 g / 7 oz white melon
250 g / 9 oz lean pork
1½ teaspoons cornflour
½ teaspoon salt
1 teaspoon black pepper
1 tablespoon light soy sauce
600 ml / 1 pint chicken stock *(see left)*

PREPARATION
In a bowl, soak the mushrooms in boiling water to cover. When it has cooled down, drain the mushrooms and dice them.
Dice the melon and pork.
Mix the cornflour with the salt and pepper and then mix to a paste with the soy sauce. Season the pork with this paste.

COOKING
In a large pan, bring the chicken stock to the boil and add the diced melon and mushroom. Continue to simmer for 15 minutes. Add the seasoned pork and simmer for 7 minutes more.
Serve hot.

Won Ton Wrappers

Won ton wrappers, or skins, are pieces of thin filo-like pastry, ready-cut to the right size and shape for the making of won tons. They are sold in all Oriental supermarkets, usually in large packs of 50 or 100, but they are cheap and you can freeze what you don't use.

Kambing Soup
Mutton or Lamb Soup

1 kg / 2 lb boned leg of mutton or lamb
8 garlic cloves
10-cm / 4-inch piece of ginger, peeled
2 onions, chopped and pounded
½ teaspoon whole cloves
10-cm / 4-inch piece of cinnamon
1 teaspoon cumin seeds
1 teaspoon fennel seeds
1 teaspoon cardamom pods
3 tablespoons cornflour
1 tablespoon oil
4 stalks of celery, chopped
3 tablespoons soy sauce
3 tomatoes, halved
8 sprigs of coriander, for garnish
crispy onion flakes *(buy packets at Chinese markets)*, for garnish

Preparation
Trim off all fat from the mutton or lamb.
Mix the garlic, ginger and onion.
Wrap the spices in a little square of muslin and tie up securely.
In a small bowl, mix the cornflour to a paste with a little water.

Cooking
In a large heavy-based saucepan, heat the oil over a low heat.
Add the mutton or lamb with the garlic mixture and stir-fry for 10 minutes.
Add enough water to cover (about 3 small cups), the bag of spices and the celery. Bring to the boil, lower the heat and simmer until the meat is tender, about 1 hour. Add the soy sauce, tomato and cornflour paste. Stir well for a minute or two. Serve hot, garnished with coriander and onion flakes.

Kai Tom Ka
Chicken and Coconut Soup

150 g / 5 oz skinless chicken breast
1 stalk of lemon grass *(see page 48)*
2.5-cm / 1-inch piece of galangal *(see page 25)*, peeled
4 lime leaves *(see below)*
600 ml / 1 pint chicken stock *(see page 19)*
1 level teaspoon salt
½ teaspoon light brown sugar
juice of 1 whole lime
10 sprigs of basil
60 g / 2 oz button mushrooms
125 ml / 4 fl oz coconut milk
1 chilli, thinly sliced, for garnish

Preparation
Slice the chicken breast thinly across the grain.
Slice the mushrooms.
Bash the lemon grass and the galangal.
Remove the hard central parts of the lime leaves, then layer the leaves on top of one another, roll them up and slice the roll across to shred the leaves as finely as you can.

Cooking
In a large pan, bring stock to the boil. Add salt, lemon grass, galangal, sugar, lime juice, chicken, mushrooms, lime leaves and most of the basil. Bring to the boil and simmer for 5 minutes. Just before serving, remove lemon grass and galangal and stir in coconut milk. Serve garnished with the chilli and remaining basil.

Coconut milk

Coconut milk is made by soaking grated coconut flesh, or even desiccated coconut, in warm water and squeezing it out of the coconut. However, coconut milk is readily available in cans and cartons and this is very good for cooking.

Kaffir Lime

The leaves and rind of this small green, knobbly-skinned tropical citrus fruit are used to impart a sourness and lemon verbena-like flavour to many Southeast Asian dishes. The limes can be bought fresh in most Oriental food stores. The distinctively shaped fresh leaves (looking like two leaves joined end to end) and curled-up dried leaves are also available. A kaffir lime has very little juice in it, so when a recipe specifies lime juice, this is always from an ordinary smooth-skinned lime.

Herbal Soup

600 ml / 1 pint rich chicken stock *(see page 19, simmered for at least 2 hours)*
175 g / 6 oz skinless chicken breast
2 tablespoons dry white wine
¼ teaspoon black pepper
1–2 tablespoon(s) fish sauce or light soy sauce
1 tablespoon wolf berries *(kei chee, see below)*
5 sprigs of fresh coriander, chopped

PREPARATION
Slice the chicken thinly across the grain.

COOKING
In a large pan, bring the chicken stock to the boil. Add the chicken and simmer for 2 minutes, or until it is cooked through. Divide the cooked chicken between the soup bowls and then pour over some of the boiling stock.
Stir some of the white wine into each bowl, together with black pepper and fish sauce or soy sauce to taste.
Garnish with the wolf berries and coriander, and serve immediately.

Prawn Toasts

150 g / 5 oz raw fresh prawns, shelled and deveined *(see page 33)*
1 tablespoon dry white wine
1 tablespoon oyster sauce
1 teaspoon fish sauce
¼ teaspoon black pepper
¼ teaspoon garlic powder
1 tablespoon self-raising flour
½ teaspoon sugar
3 tablespoons sesame seeds
6 slices of medium-cut white bread
oil for deep-frying

PREPARATION
In a blender or food processor, mince the prawns with all the other ingredients except the sesame seeds and bread.
Remove the crusts from the bread.
With a spatula, spread the mixture on the bread and flatten it down into the bread.
Sprinkle the sesame seeds on top of the mixture and press them down.

COOKING
Heat the oil in a wok or frying pan and deep-fry the slices of bread, with the prawn-mixture side down, until golden.
Slice each piece of bread into 4 – soldiers or triangles as you wish – to serve.

Wolf Berries

These sweet little berries, looking like orangey-red raisins, are known as *kei chee* in China and their mild liquorice flavour is popular in Cantonese soups. They come from a shrub called the matrimony vine, the peppermint-flavoured leaves of which are traditionally eaten in the spring, the flowers in the summer, the berries in the autumn, and the root in the winter. The berries and leaves are increasingly easy to find in Chinese supermarkets.

Spring Rolls with Beancurd Skin

175 g / 6 oz lean pork fillet
115 g / 4 oz raw fresh prawns, shelled and deveined *(see page 33)*
60 g / 2 oz drained canned water chestnuts, finely chopped
1 small carrot, cut into matchstick strips
5 shallots
2 garlic cloves, finely chopped
2 tablespoons oyster sauce
1 tablespoon sesame oil
½ teaspoon black pepper
1 tablespoon soy sauce
pinch of salt
1 egg yolk
1½ teaspoons cornflour, plus more for sealing
packet of soft beancurd skin *(see below)*
oil for deep-frying
chilli sauce, to serve

PREPARATION

Mince the pork and prawns coarsely and put in a large bowl. Add the water chestnuts, carrot, shallots, garlic, oyster sauce, sesame oil, pepper, soy sauce, salt, egg yolk and cornflour and mix together well.

Cut the beancurd skin into pieces about 15 cm / 6 inches square. Divide the filling mixture between the beancurd-skin pieces, positioning it in the centre. Roll the skins up like cigars and seal the edges with a paste made from a little cornflour and a very little water.

COOKING

Steam the prepared spring rolls for 10 minutes in a bamboo steamer. Then deep-fry them in a wok or frying pan until golden brown, in batches if necessary.

Serve hot with chilli sauce.

Beancurd Skin

Just as its name implies, this is the firmish skim of the tofu as it is made from soya bean curds. Beancurd skin is sold in Oriental supermarkets and shops, in fairly large packs. You can, however, keep what isn't used wrapped in cling film and then in foil in the refrigerator for some weeks.

Aubergine in Hot Sauce

5 long (Oriental) aubergines
1 large red onion
4 sprigs of coriander
500 g / 1 lb tomatoes
3 garlic cloves
2 thin slices of ginger
1 whole clove
½ teaspoon black peppercorns
½ teaspoon fennel seeds
1 red chilli
2 tablespoons oil
salt

PREPARATION

Top and tail the aubergines, then cut them lengthwise into
6 slices. Soak the slices in a bowl of cold water until ready to
use them further.

Chop the red onion finely and chop the coriander for garnish.
Halve the tomatoes, remove their seeds and then coarsely chop
the flesh.

Using a pestle and mortar, pound to a paste the garlic, ginger,
clove, peppercorns, fennel seeds and chilli. Add salt to taste.

COOKING

Preheat a hot grill.

Heat the oil in a wok or frying pan and add the paste and the
chopped tomatoes. Stir-fry over a moderate heat until
aromatic, about 5 minutes.

Drain the aubergine slices, pat dry with paper
towels and arrange them on a round pie
dish in a radiating flower shape.

Pour over the sauce and grill for
about 20 minutes, until just
nicely browned.

Chicken Satay

500 g / 1 lb skinless chicken breast
10 cm / 4 inches of base end of a stalk of lemon grass *(see
page 48)*
2 teaspoons ground coriander
1 teaspoon ground galangal *(see below)*
1 teaspoon ground turmeric
2 tablespoons sugar
1 teaspoon salt
2 tablespoons soy sauce
1 tablespoon ketjap manis *(see page 92)*
12 satay sticks, about 10-15 cm / 4-6 inches long

PREPARATION

Slice the chicken into strips across the grain.
Slice the lemon grass and chop or grind it very finely.
Put the sliced chicken in a mixing bowl and add the lemon grass
and all the other ingredients. Mix well with a spatula or your
hands. Set aside for 30 minutes to 1 hour to marinate.
Thread the slices of chicken on the satay sticks.

COOKING

Grill or barbecue the chicken satays on a high heat for up to
5 minutes on both sides, until well browned all over.

Galangal

Also known as *galangale* and *laos* or
lengkuas in Indonesia and *ka* in
Thailand, this is a rhizome like
ginger which has a similar flavour
although with a more powerful,
sour overtone.

In fact, the Thais prefer it to
ginger in their cooking. The
fresh rhizome is available
from good Oriental
supermarkets and shops.
Treated like ginger, it is
peeled then sliced, cut into
matchstick shreds or grated.
Dried slices and powder are
also available.

Stir-fried Asparagus

275 g / 10 oz asparagus
1 tablespoon sesame oil
1 garlic clove, sliced
2 tablespoons dry white wine
1 tablespoon oyster sauce

PREPARATION

Trim off hard bases of the asparagus stalks. Halve them if long, but leave baby asparagus whole.

COOKING

Heat the oil in a wok or frying pan, then add the garlic and the asparagus and stir-fry together for about 5 minutes. Stir in the white wine and oyster sauce, and serve hot.

Sambal Mussels

500 g / 1 lb mussels
2 red chillies
4 garlic cloves
1 stalk of lemon grass *(see page 48)*
1 large onion
2 teaspoons tamarind pulp *(see page 38)*
2 tablespoons oil
¼ teaspoon shrimp paste *(blachan, see page 18)*
2 tablespoons sugar
½ teaspoon salt

PREPARATION

Scrub the mussels well and drain. Discard any that stay open when handled.
Grind the chillies, garlic, lemon grass and onion to a paste.
Soak the tamarind pulp in warm water for 5 minutes, squeeze well and drain. Discard the pulp.

COOKING

Heat the oil in a wok or frying pan (use only stainless steel or non-stick as you are using tamarind) and stir-fry the ground chilli mixture and the shrimp paste for 5 minutes.
Add the tamarind juice and mussels and cook over a high heat until all the mussels have opened.
Add sugar and salt to taste and serve hot.

Nancy's 10 Stir-frying Commandments

PS Don't call me if anything burns!

1 Don't waste money on expensive fancy woks, buy good cheap ones from Asian markets (they can be replaced regularly)!

2 Get all your ingredients prepared for the wok ahead of time and put them in bowls, grouping all those that are added at each stage!

3 Don't do this preparation too far ahead, do it just before cooking or your ingredients will lose their freshness!

4 Use any good vegetable oils that take heat well, like groundnut or corn oil (I always use sunflower oil). If you use olive oil, it will taste quite different!

5 Get the wok and the oil nice and hot before adding any food!

6 Don't panic when the oil gets smoky and the food sizzles! Lose heart and lower the heat and you won't get crisp results.

7 Keep stirring all the time – that's why it's called stir-frying!

8 Don't daydream when you're stir-frying, it needs concentration and attention (you are allowed to think of your lover, though)!

9 However, you can wok and tok!

10 Get cooked food out of the wok quickly so it doesn't go soggy!

Prawnography

Fish and Shellfish

Always buy the best and freshest of fish and other seafood – look for clear eyes in fish, and shellfish that smell sweetly of the sea and feel heavy for their size. It's best to buy live shellfish, as you can then be sure of their freshness. If using frozen prawns, let them defrost to get rid of any ice glaze and then rinse them well under cold running water to sweeten them up before cooking.

The secret of cooking fish and shellfish is to get the pan nice and hot and to cook them only very briefly. Texture is everything in seafood – and even slight overcooking ruins them.

Curry Prawns

500 g / 1 lb raw prawns
5-mm / ¼-inch piece of fresh turmeric *(see page 66)*, peeled
1 large onion
2 tablespoons oil
½ teaspoon chilli powder
½ teaspoon ground coriander
¼ teaspoon ground cumin
¼ teaspoon fennel seeds
125 ml / 4 fl oz coconut milk
salt to taste
sugar to taste
6 sprigs of fresh coriander, for garnish

PREPARATION

Shell and devein the prawns *(see below)*.
In a blender or food processor, separately grind the fresh turmeric and the onion.

COOKING

In a heavy-based saucepan, heat the oil and fry the onion for a minute. Add the turmeric, chilli powder, ground coriander, cumin and fennel seeds. Stir well until lightly browned.
Add the prawns and cook on high heat until they turn pink.
Add the coconut milk, with salt and sugar to taste.
Serve hot, garnished with coriander sprigs.

French Beans with Prawn Lemak

175 g / 6 oz raw prawns
1 red chilli
1 green chilli
1 medium onion
5-cm / 2-inch piece of galangal *(see page 25)*, peeled
250 g / 9 oz French beans
2 tablespoons oil
¼ teaspoon shrimp paste *(optional – blachan, see page 18)*
125 ml / 4 fl oz coconut milk
salt to taste
sugar to taste

PREPARATION

Shell and devein the prawns *(see below)*.
Thinly slice the chillies, onion and galangal.
Top and tail the French beans and cut them across into half.

COOKING

Heat the oil in a wok or frying pan, and fry the chillies, onions and galangal for 2 minutes.
Add half a small cup of water and the French beans and shrimp paste, if you are using it. Cook over high heat for a further 3 minutes.
Add the prawns and stir-fry for 2–3 minutes more.
Just before serving, add the coconut milk and salt and sugar to taste. Serve hot.

Shelling and deveining prawns

The heads of prawns are usually removed and then the shell prised off the tail meat. You can leave the end fin on the tail for a better appearance. In larger prawns, the intestinal tract must be removed before cooking. Simply cut into the flesh along the back of the prawn (outer curve) and this should reveal a long black 'thread'. Make sure you cut out as much of this as you can. If the prawns are still in their shells, it can still be reached by cutting through the unprotected underside.

Sambal Prawns

175 g / 6 oz raw fresh prawns
10 red chillies
3 shallots
1-cm / ½-inch piece of galangal *(see page 25)*, peeled
2.5-cm / 1-inch piece of ginger, peeled
2 lime leaves *(see page 20)*
1 green mango *(see below)*
2 tablespoons oil
4 garlic cloves
½ teaspoon salt
1½ teaspoons sugar
125 ml / 4 fl oz coconut milk

Preparation

Shell and devein the prawns *(see page 33)*.
Slice the chillies, shallots, galangal and ginger into matchstick shreds.
Remove the hard stalks from the lime leaves, layer them on top of each other, roll up and cut across into the finest shreds you can manage. Peel the mango, remove the flesh from around the stone and cut it into cubes

Cooking

Heat the oil in a wok or frying pan and fry the garlic and the shallots, then add the prawns and continue stir-frying until they just turn pink.
Add the galangal, ginger, lime leaves, mango, chillies, salt, sugar and coconut milk. Stir-fry until aromatic, about 5 minutes.
Serve hot.

Green Mangoes

Unripe mangoes are popular as a vegetable in the cooking of Southeast Asia. They are available in many ethnic street markets and in some Oriental shops. They do tend to be quite large and, as they are sold by weight, quite expensive.

Lobster Nancy's Style

2 live lobsters, each weighing about 675 g / 1½ lb
5-cm / 2-inch piece of ginger, peeled
2 garlic cloves
1½ tablespoons cornflour
2 tablespoons oil
½ cup fish or chicken stock or water
1 teaspoon fish sauce
2 teaspoons crushed black bean sauce *(see page 64)*
1 tablespoon sugar
4 tablespoons dry white wine

FOR GARNISH
2 spring onions, chopped
3-4 sprigs of coriander, chopped
1 red chilli, thinly sliced

Preparation

You first need to kill the lobsters humanely: there is a point marked by two lines that cross at right angles where the head meets the body, and piercing down through the point with a long sharp knife will dispatch the creature swiftly and fairly painlessly (the body will continue to move, so be careful, but it will then be clinically dead). Cut each lobster into 2 with a pair of kitchen scissors or poultry shears. Cut the tail into 2 horizontally and cut the head into 4 pieces (a total of 12 pieces).
Slice the ginger into matchstick strips and chop the garlic finely. Mix the cornflour with a little water.

Cooking

Heat the oil in a wok or frying pan and fry the garlic and ginger until aromatic.
Add the lobster and stir-fry for 1 minute, then add the stock or water and cover. Boil rapidly for 10-15 minutes over a high heat. Remove the lobster and arrange on a serving plate.
Add the fish sauce, black bean sauce, sugar, cornflour paste and white wine to the wok or pan, give a good stir over the heat and pour the sauce over the lobster to serve.
Garnish with the spring onions, coriander and chilli.

Prawn and Vegetable Fritters

175 g / 6 oz raw fresh prawns
60 g / 2 oz sweet potato
4 spring onions
2 sprigs of fresh coriander
100 g / 3½ oz plain flour
2 eggs
salt to taste
½ teaspoon black pepper
85 g / 3 oz beansprouts
oil for deep-frying
chilli sauce, to serve

PREPARATION
Shell and devein the prawns *(see page 33)*.

Slice the sweet potato into matchstick strips.
Chop the spring onion and the coriander finely.
Sieve the flour into a mixing bowl. Add the eggs, spring onions, coriander, salt and pepper. Sir in half a small cup of water and mix well to produce a batter. Leave to stand for 30 minutes.

COOKING
Heat the oil in a wok or frying pan.
Dip a 5-cm / 2-inch ladle into the hot oil briefly to warm it, then pour 1 tablespoon of batter into the warm ladle. Tip from side to side so that the batter completely covers the interior and forms a shell. Add some sweet potato and beansprouts, followed by a few prawns, then pour 1 or 2 tablespoons of batter on top.
Dip the ladle in the hot oil and leave it until the fritter floats free and is golden brown. Continue until all ingredients are used.
Serve the fritters piping hot as soon as all are cooked, with some chilli sauce as a dip.

Udang Salad
Prawn Salad

60 g / 2 oz raw prawns
juice of 1 lime
1 small carrot
1 small onion, thinly sliced
10 thin slices of cucumber
1 tablespoon oil
1 garlic clove, chopped
1 tablespoon fish sauce
½ teaspoon sugar
2 teaspoons sesame oil
2 teaspoons sesame seeds, for garnish
2 spring onions, sliced, for garnish

PREPARATION
Shell and devein the prawns *(see page 33)*. Put them in a bowl,
pour the lime juice over them and toss until well coated.
Cut the carrot into matchstick strips and put into a salad bowl
with the onion and cucumber slices.

COOKING
Heat the oil and stir-fry the prawns.
Transfer to the salad bowl. Add the chopped garlic, fish sauce,
sugar and sesame oil and mix well.
Garnish with the sesame seeds and spring onions to serve.

Udang Lemak
Prawns in a Rich Coconut Sauce

18 raw prawns
1 teaspoon sugar
2 teaspoons fish sauce
1 beef tomato
1 large onion
1 tablespoon oil
1 tablespoon chilli sauce
2 tablespoons coconut powder

PREPARATION
Shell and devein the prawns *(see page 33)*.
Dissolve the sugar in the fish sauce.
Slice the tomato and the onion.

COOKING
In a very hot wok or frying pan, heat the oil and add the onion
and tomato. Stir-fry for a few minutes, then add the prawns and
cook until they turn pink.
Add the chilli sauce with the sweetened fish sauce and bring to
the boil.
Finally, stir in the coconut powder to serve.

Garlic Prawns in the Shell

500 g / 1 lb raw prawns in their shells
8 garlic cloves
2 chillies
2 spring onions
2 sprigs of coriander
1 tablespoon oil
4 tablespoons tomato ketchup
1 teaspoon sugar
about 2 tablespoons fish sauce

PREPARATION

Wash the prawns and devein them *(see page 33)*.
Pound the garlic.
Grind the chillies.
Chop the spring onions and coriander.

COOKING

Heat the oil in a wok or frying pan over a high heat and add the garlic and chilli. Stir-fry for 1 minute.
Add the prawns over a low heat and cook until the prawns have changed to a light pink colour and they curl nicely.
Stir in the tomato ketchup, sugar, spring onions, coriander and fish sauce to taste before serving.

Sweet-and-sour Prawns in Tamarind Juice

This is one of Indonesia's very high-class dishes.

500 g /1 lb raw prawns in their shells
30 g / 1 oz tamarind pulp *(see below)*
5 garlic cloves
2 tablespoons oil
2 tablespoons palm sugar *(see page 90)*
1 teaspoon black pepper
4 tablespoons ketjap manis *(see page 92)*
¼ cucumber, sliced, for garnish

PREPARATION

Clean the prawns and devein them *(see page 33)*.
Soak the tamarind in 3 tablespoons of hot water and squeeze to extract the juice. Discard the pulp.
Pound the garlic.

COOKING

In a hot stainless-steel or non-stick wok or frying pan, heat the oil and fry the garlic in it.
Next add the prawns, the palm sugar and the black pepper. Continue to stir-fry over high heat for 5 minutes.
Add the tamarind juice and ketjap manis, and stir-fry for 2 minutes more.
Transfer to a serving plate and garnish with the cucumber to serve.

Tamarind

The pods of the tamarind tree (*asam* in Southeast Asia) have been used as a flavouring in India and Asia for centuries. Valued for its sweet-and-sour fruity flavour (familiar in the West in many bottled sauces), tamarind is normally sold as a sticky mass of partly dried pods and pulp. To use it, simply break off the right-sized piece from the block and soak it in hot water for about 10 minutes, then squeeze it to get the brown juice from the pulp. The pulp is then discarded and the liquid used. Tamarind liquid tends to react with metal, so use only ceramic or glass bowls and stainless-steel or non-stick utensils when cooking with it.

Sayur Campong Udang
Village Vegetable Prawns

115 g / 4 oz raw fresh prawns
400 g / 14 oz canned banana flowers *(see below)*, drained
1 small sweet potato
1 medium carrot
115 g / 4 oz cabbage
115 g / 4 oz yam leaves or spinach
1 chilli
1 onion
2.5-cm / 1-inch piece of fresh turmeric *(see page 66)*, peeled
very little shrimp paste *(blachan, see page 18)*
125 ml / 4 fl oz coconut cream or milk
1-2 teaspoon(s) salt

PREPARATION
Shell and devein the prawns *(see page 33)*.
Remove the hard stems from the banana flowers.
Cut the potato, carrot and cabbage into bite-sized pieces.
Blend the chilli, onion, turmeric and blachan to a paste.

COOKING
Add a small cupful of water to the blended paste and bring to the boil, then simmer for 10 minutes.
Add the sweet potato and carrot and cook for about 2 minutes.
Then add the cabbage, yam leaves or spinach and the banana flowers, and cook for 5 minutes more.
Lastly, add the coconut cream or milk with the prawns and salt to taste. Cook for 3 minutes.
Serve hot with boiled rice.

Banana flowers

The heart-shaped flower of the banana plant, *jantung pisang*, is cooked and eaten as a vegetable in Indonesia and other parts of Southeast Asia. If you can get them fresh, they are wonderfully tasty; otherwise canned banana flowers are available from some Oriental supermarkets.

Sotong Lemak Serai
Squid with Lemon Grass and Coconut

225 g / 8 oz fresh squid *(ask your fishmonger to clean the squid for you)*
½ stalk of lemon grass *(see page 48)*
1 tablespoon oil
1 tablespoon fish sauce
4 tablespoons coconut milk
1 chilli, chopped

PREPARATION
Rinse the squid, pat dry with paper towels and cut some into rounds and others into diamond shapes. Leave the tentacles whole.
Bash the lemon grass.

COOKING
Heat the oil in a wok or frying pan over a high heat and stir-fry the lemon grass, squid and fish sauce for about 2 minutes. Remove and discard the lemon grass, add the coconut milk and chilli and serve.

Tamarind Vegetables with Prawns

175 g / 6 oz raw fresh prawns
115 g / 4 oz long beans *(see below)*
175 g / 6 oz cabbage
115 g / 4 oz carrots
225 g / ½ lb aubergine
1 tablespoon tamarind pulp *(see page 38)*
7.5-cm / 3-inch piece of lemon grass *(see page 48)*
2.5-cm / 1-inch piece of galangal *(see page 25)*, peeled
4–5 candlenuts *(see below)*
2.5-cm / 1-inch piece of turmeric *(see page 66)*, peeled
1 large onion
¼ teaspoon shrimp paste *(blachan, see page 18)*
3 tablespoons oil
salt to taste
sugar to taste

PREPARATION
Shell and devein the prawns *(see page 33)*.
Cut all the vegetables into bite-sized pieces.
Soak the tamarind in a small cup of water and squeeze to extract the juice, then discard the pulp.
Grind the lemon grass, galangal, candlenuts, turmeric and onion into a paste and add the shrimp paste.

COOKING
Heat the oil in a stainless-steel wok or frying pan and fry the flavouring paste for 5 minutes.
Stir in the tamarind juice and simmer for a further 5 minutes.
Add the vegetables and simmer for 10 minutes.
Stir in salt and sugar to taste.
Add the prawns and stir-fry for 2 minutes before serving.

Candlenuts

Known as *kemiri* in Indonesia, these large oily nuts are about the size of a whole walnut. The outer shell is so hard that they are normally sold ready-shelled, and sometimes large nuts are broken into pieces (count them as one nut). Packets of candlenuts are obtainable from most good Oriental markets. They should not be eaten raw as they are slightly toxic, though perfectly safe once cooked. If you can't find candlenuts, some of the same effect can be achieved by using macadamia nuts.

Long Beans

Also called 'yard-long' or 'snake' beans, these are a variety of green bean that can actually grow up to a metre in length. They are available in many good Oriental – especially Thai – stores. When you buy them, snap a bean with your fingers; if it snaps easily, it is fresh. If you need to cut it with knife, the beans are old and quite fibrous. Young French beans make a good substitute.

Shallow-fried Stuffed Salmon Rolls

500 g / 1 lb skinless salmon fillets
5 dried Chinese mushrooms
1 carrot
4 thin slices of ginger
1 spring onion
1 tablespoon cornflour
5 tablespoons self-raising flour
2 tablespoons fish sauce
1 teaspoon black pepper
2 tablespoons sesame oil
oil for shallow-frying
chilli sauce, to serve
ketjap manis *(see page 92)*, to serve

PREPARATION

Cut the salmon fillets into as many pieces, each about 10x5 cm / 4x2 inches and about 1 cm / ½ inch thick, as possible.
Place the mushrooms in a heatproof bowl and pour over boiling water to cover. Leave for 10 minutes. When cool, drain and slice thinly.
Slice the carrot, the ginger and the spring onion into matchstick strips.
Sieve the cornflour and self-raising flour together.
In a large mixing bowl, mix the sliced mushrooms, carrots and the fish sauce, pepper, spring onion, ginger and sesame oil together with a spatula.

COOKING

Lay each piece of salmon on a chopping board. Put a tablespoonful of the mixture in the centre and roll it up. Secure it with a wooden cocktail stick and then roll it in the flour.
Shallow-fry the stuffed salmon rolls, in batches if necessary, moving them about so that they cook on all sides, for about 5 minutes, until golden brown all over.
Serve with chilli sauce and ketjap manis.

Sambal Ikan Goreng
Fish Sambal

1 whole fish, such as red tilapia or mackerel, weighing about 675 g / 1½ lb
1-2 tablespoon(s) flour
3 sprigs of coriander
2 tablespoons oil
1 garlic clove
1 small onion
2-3 tablespoons sweet soy sauce

PREPARATION

Clean, scale and gut the fish. Cut off the head if you prefer. Pat dry with paper towels.
Using a sharp knife, slash either side of the fish with a lattice of cuts to let flavours and heat penetrate the flesh.
Rub the fish on both sides with the flour.
Chop the coriander.

COOKING

Heat the oil in a wok or frying pan.
Fry the fish, turning from time to time, for about 5 minutes in total on each side, until both sides are brown. Transfer to a warm serving plate.
Add the garlic, onion and soy sauce to the oil remaining in the wok or frying pan and stir-fry for about 2 minutes, until aromatic.
Pour over the fish, garnish with the coriander and serve.

Chilli Sauce

A wide variety of chilli sauces is available, ranging from fairly mild in chilli heat – often mellowed by the inclusion of red sweet peppers and tomatoes – to pretty pungent. Try one or two to find a sauce that suits your taste. They are generally used for meat and fish dishes, and in marinades and barbecue sauces. If you haven't got any, a few drops of Tabasco or some chilli oil or powder can produce roughly the same effect in cooking, or add one of these to hoisin sauce for a chilli sauce dip or dressing.

Spicy Seafood Omelette

60 g / 2 oz raw fresh prawns
2 spring onions
2 sprigs of fresh coriander
1 fresh chilli
1 small red onion
4 large eggs
½ teaspoon cornflour
2 tablespoons fish sauce
¼ teaspoon black pepper
1 tablespoon oil
60 g / 2 oz crab meat

PREPARATION
Shell and devein the prawns *(see page 33)*.
Chop the spring onions, coriander and chilli. Slice the red onion.
In a bowl, beat the eggs with the cornflour, fish sauce and
pepper.

COOKING
Preheat the grill to high.
Heat the oil in a flameproof frying pan over a moderate heat and
add the onion, prawns and crab meat. Stir-fry for 2 minutes.
Add the egg mixture and mix well. Fry until the bottom is set and
lightly browned.
Place the pan under the grill to brown the top.
Serve garnished with the spring onions, coriander and chilli.

Otar Otar
Spicy Fish Cake

300 g / 10½ oz skinless cod fillets
1 stalk of lemon grass *(see page 48)*
1 tablespoon desiccated coconut
175 ml / 6 fl oz coconut milk
1 tablespoon cornflour
whites of 2 eggs
1 teaspoon ground turmeric
3 sprigs of sweet basil
1 teaspoon salt
1 teaspoon sugar
2–3 banana leaves *(see below)*

PREPARATION
Mince the cod, but not too finely – you still want to keep some of
the fish's texture.
Grind the lemon grass in a blender or food processor.
In a large bowl, mix the fish and lemon grass together with all
the other ingredients except the banana leaves.
Cut the banana leaves into pieces about 15 cm / 6 inches square.
Put a tablespoonful of mixture in each of the pieces of banana
leaf. Roll up into parcels and secure either end with a wooden
cocktail stick.

COOKING
Grill or barbecue the fish-cake parcels for 10-15 minutes, until
cooked and lightly browned.

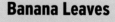

Banana Leaves

Banana leaves are used in
many parts of the tropics as
both disposable plates for
food and to wrap food for
cooking. Food cooked in banana-
leaf parcels does benefit from an
indefinable added flavour imparted by
the leaves. You can often find banana
leaves in ethnic markets. The large
leaves are usually torn in half along the
mid-ribs, which are removed and
discarded. Warming the leaves over a
flame will make them more pliable.

Fish Stuffed with Chillies

1 whole mackerel
4 fairly large chillies
1½ teaspoons salt
¼ teaspoon shrimp paste *(blachan, see page 18)*
2 tablespoons oil

PREPARATION
Clean the fish, scaling and gutting it.
Grind the chillies finely and mix with the salt and blachan.
Stuff this chilli paste into the cavity of the fish.

COOKING
Heat the oil in a wok or frying pan over a moderate heat and fry
the fish for 5 minutes on each side or until cooked (the flesh
flakes readily when pierced with a fork).
Serve hot with plain boiled rice.

Stewed Fish with Mushrooms in a Clay Pot

500 g / 1 lb skinless fillets of fish, such as cod, halibut or
monkfish
250 g / 9 oz dried Chinese mushrooms
5 garlic cloves
5 spring onions
2 teaspoons cornflour
2 tablespoons oil
4 tablespoons light soy sauce
1 teaspoon black pepper

PREPARATION
Cut the fish into 4 equal pieces.
Place the Chinese mushrooms in a small heatproof bowl, and
pour over boiling water. Leave for 20 minutes. Drain and slice the
rehydrated mushrooms.
Pound the garlic.
Chop each spring onion into 4 lengths.
Mix the cornflour to a paste with 1½ small cups of water.

COOKING
Heat the oil in a wok or frying pan and fry the mushrooms for
5 minutes. Add the garlic and stir-fry quickly for a minute or two.
Transfer mushrooms and garlic to a clay pot.
Add the cornflour mixture, soy sauce and black pepper. Bring to
the boil.
Lay the pieces of fish on top of the mushrooms and sprinkle the
spring onions over them. Bring to the boil over a high heat.
Cover, remove from the heat and leave for at least 10 minutes or
until ready to serve.
Serve hot.

Clay Pots

In Southeast Asia it is a fairly common practice to slow-cook
dishes in clay crocks set in the embers of the fire. The pots
usually have wide rims so that the cover seals it tightly.

47

Fish Curry

1 kg / 2¼ lb boneless fillets of white fish, such as cod or halibut
1 large aubergine
1 large red onion
2.5-cm / 1-inch piece of ginger, peeled
3 garlic cloves
2 tablespoons oil
1 teaspoon dried fenugreek
1 teaspoon poppy seeds
1 teaspoon curry powder
1 tablespoon tamarind pulp *(see page 38)*
1 large tomato, sliced
4 whole green chillies
salt

PREPARATION

Rinse the fish, pat dry and cut into portion-sized pieces.
Soak the tamarind pulp in 1 small cup of water, squeeze and drain, then discard the tamarind pulp.
Cut the aubergine into bite-sized pieces.
Grind the red onion, ginger and garlic.

COOKING

Heat the oil in a stainless-steel or non-stick wok or frying pan.
Add the fenugreek and poppy seeds and quickly stir-fry.
Add the ginger, garlic, onion and curry powder. Stir well for 5 minutes over a medium heat without burning.
Add the tamarind juice and bring back to the boil. With the contents of the pan bubbling, add the aubergine, tomatoes, chillies and salt to taste. Add the fish, cover and simmer gently for 10 minutes. Serve with plain boiled rice.

Lemon Grass

Several similar types of tropical grass are sold as lemon grass, all having strongly citrus-flavoured oils in them. The stalks, looking a bit like emaciated spring onions, are usually pounded first to encourage the oils to come forth. The outer part of the stalk is fairly inedible, so if a whole stalk is used it is normally removed prior to serving. Alternatively, the outer stalk can first be peeled off to reveal the short softish inner core at the root end, which is chopped and added for incorporation in a dish. Also know as *sereh* in Southeast Asia, lemon grass stalks are now readily available from better supermarkets. In Indonesia, young girls are sent to harvest lemon grass, as legend has it that the best flavours come from grass picked by virgins.

Goreng Assam Fish

Fried Fish with Tamarind

1 whole red snapper or tilapia, weighing about 675 g / 1½ lb
1 red chilli
1 onion
5-cm / 2-inch length of lemon grass *(see below)*
2.5-cm / 1-inch piece of galangal *(see page 25)*, peeled
1-cm / ½-inch piece of fresh turmeric *(see page 66)*, peeled
¼ teaspoon shrimp paste *(blachan, see page 18)*
3 candlenuts *(see page 41)*
2 teaspoons tamarind pulp *(see page 38)*
2 tomatoes
6 okra *(optional)*
2 tablespoons oil
sugar to taste
salt to taste

PREPARATION

Gut the fish and scale, then wash well. Cut 3 parallel slits on either side of the fish to let the flavours and heat penetrate.
Chop the chilli coarsely.
Chop the onion finely.
Grind the lemon grass, galangal, turmeric, shrimp paste and candlenuts finely to a paste.
Soak the tamarind pulp in 1 small cup of water, squeeze and drain, then discard the tamarind pulp.
Cut the tomatoes into halves.
Top and tail the okra.

COOKING

Heat the oil in a stainless-steel or non-stick frying pan and fry the aromatic paste with the onion and chilli until pungent.
Then add the tamarind juice and simmer for 10 minutes.
Add the tomatoes and okra and continue to stir.
Finally add the fish, sugar and salt to taste. Simmer for 10 minutes.
Serve hot.

Put that in your wok and cook it!

Lemon Fish

275 g / 10 oz fillets of white fish, such as cod or halibut
1 large lemon
1 garlic clove
6 thin slices of ginger
2 tablespoons sugar
1 teaspoon cornflour
salt to taste
115 g / 4 oz self-raising flour
1 teaspoon garlic powder
½ teaspoon black pepper
oil for deep-frying

PREPARATION
Cut the fish into bite-sized cubes.
Squeeze the juice from the lemon.
Slice the garlic.

COOKING
Start by making the sauce: in a stainless-steel pot, heat a little
oil and fry the garlic, ginger, lemon juice, sugar, cornflour and
salt to taste until aromatic. Add just enough water to dilute to a
sauce with a coating consistency. Leave to simmer for 5 minutes.
While the sauce is simmering, sieve the flour into a mixing bowl
and add the salt, garlic powder and pepper. Add about 100 ml /
3½ fl oz water, just enough to produce a thick batter consistency.
Whisk vigorously until smooth.
Dip the pieces of fish one by one into the batter and deep-fry
until golden brown.
Pour the sauce over the fried fish to serve.

Steamed Fish with Ginger and Spring Onion

1 whole sea bass, weighing about 675 g / 1½ lb
1 tablespoon salt
5-cm / 2-inch piece of ginger, peeled
2 spring onions
2 sprigs of coriander
2 tablespoons soy sauce
1 tablespoon oil

PREPARATION
Gut and scale the fish. Rub it all over with the salt and
then rinse. Slit a diamond lattice of cuts on both sides to
let flavours and heat penetrate the flesh.
Slice the ginger into matchstick strips.
Slice the spring onions finely.
Chop the coriander.

COOKING
Line the cavity of the fish with half the spring onions
and half the ginger and place it on a plate.
Set this over a high heat in a bamboo steamer and
steam the fish for 20 minutes.
Remove the fish from the steamer, put on a serving
plate and pour the soy sauce over it.
In a hot wok, heat the oil and stir-fry the remaining
ginger until aromatic. Sprinkle this over the fish.
Garnish with the coriander and remaining spring onions.

Nancy's 7 Steps to Successful Steaming

Remember, no matter how much you steam it, it won't get crusty!

1 You don't need expensive special saucepans – the tiered bamboo steamers you can find at Oriental supermarkets are very cheap.

2 You can use a bamboo steamer with any pan that's large enough, but preferably one that gives it a nice fit (just to keep the kitchen from filling with steam!)

3 Find a plate that just fits inside the steamer, but leaves enough space around the edge for the steam to circulate.

4 Make sure there is plenty of water in the pan, but that it doesn't quite touch the plate.

5 Get your water to a really good rolling boil and keep it that way throughout the cooking process. (When steaming is lengthy, top up if necessary with more boiling water from the kettle!)

6 Don't be tempted to keep lifting the lid for a peek at the food, otherwise you'll lose the steam and slow down the cooking.

7 'Hot', 'steamy' and 'fast' (eh, Ben?) are the steaming watchwords – especially when cooking fish and shellfish.

Chicken lickin'

Poultry Dishes

Poultry is so versatile and really takes to the Southeast Asian flavourings. Wings, thighs and drumsticks are generally cooked whole, with thighs and drumsticks slashed deeply so the flavourings and heat can penetrate the flesh more easily. Chicken breast meat is usually skinned and cut into slices or cubes. As breast meat tends to be dry, be careful not to overcook it when stir-frying. The meat should just be opaque and feel bouncy when prodded with a fingertip (and any juices run clear rather than pink). The recipes for whole chickens usually call for a small bird, about 1.25 kg / 2½ lb in weight, more like the scrawny creatures you'll find for sale in the East.

Ayam Campong
Indonesian Chicken Curry

1 small chicken, about 1.25 kg / 2½ lb
6 candlenuts *(see page 41)*
1-cm / ½-inch piece of galangal *(see page 25)*, peeled
5-cm / 2-inch piece of fresh turmeric *(see page 66)*, peeled
4 shallots or 1 large onion
1-cm / ½-inch piece of ginger, peeled
2 garlic cloves
1 stalk of lemon grass *(see page 48)*
1 tablespoons oil
1 teaspoon salt
1 teaspoon sugar
225 ml / 8 fl oz coconut milk

PREPARATION
Cut the chicken into 16 pieces *(see below)*.
Blend the candlenuts, galangal, turmeric, shallots, ginger and
garlic to a paste.
Bash the lemon grass.

COOKING
Heat the oil in a wok or frying pan and stir-fry the blended paste
with the lemon grass, salt and sugar for 5 minutes.
Add the chicken with 1 small cup of water, cover and simmer for
20 minutes.
Stir in the coconut milk, remove the lemon grass and bring to the
boil briefly before serving.

Ayam Goreng Jakarta
Fried Chicken Jakarta-style

This recipe comes from our friend Lily, with whom we stay
when we are in Indonesia.

1 small chicken, about 1.25 kg / 2½ lb
6 candlenuts *(see page 41)*
7.5-cm / 3-inch piece of fresh turmeric *(see page 66)*, peeled
2.5-cm / 1-inch piece of galangal *(see page 25)*, peeled
4 shallots or 1 large onion
2.5-cm / 1-inch piece of ginger, peeled
5 lime leaves *(see page 20)*
1 stalk of lemon grass *(see page 48)*
1 tablespoon coriander seeds
1½ teaspoons salt
1 teaspoon sugar
oil for deep-frying

PREPARATION
Cut the chicken into 8-10 pieces *(see below)*.
Grind all the remaining ingredients except the oil into a paste.
Coat the chicken with the paste and leave to marinate for
2 hours or more.

COOKING
Deep-fry the pieces of chicken in hot oil, in batches if necessary,
until golden brown and serve.

Cutting Up a Chicken

Usually in Western cooking a chicken is cut up into 2 breast
fillets, the 2 wings and the 2 legs to produce 6 pieces in all, or the
legs are divided into thighs and drumsticks to give 8 pieces. To
get 10 or 12 pieces simply divide each breast fillet into 2 or 3
pieces. For 14 or 16, chop the thighs and drumsticks into 2 pieces
each and then divide the breast into 2 or 3 pieces. For 18 or 20,
divide each of the wings into 2 and cut the breast into 3 or 4
pieces. Big sturdy kitchen scissors or poultry shears are best for
the job, or just a good sharp heavy knife. Remember to keep the
carcass and all the trimmings for stock.

Barbecued Chicken with Coriander Root

4 medium skinless chicken breasts
small bunch of coriander, with stalks and roots
4 tablespoons fish sauce
1 teaspoon sugar
1 teaspoon black pepper
1 garlic clove, chopped
½ teaspoon salt

PREPARATION
Clean the chicken and trim off any excess fat.
Wash the coriander, including the roots (rinse these well, as you would do with leeks) and stalks.
Purée the coriander leaves, roots and stalks, reserving a few leaves for garnish. Add the fish sauce, sugar, black pepper, garlic and salt.
Put the chicken in a large bowl and add the blended flavourings. Toss well to coat and leave for 2 hours or more to marinate.

COOKING
Cook the chicken under a preheated hot grill or over a hot barbecue.
Slice the cooked chicken with a sharp knife or scissors and serve garnished with the reserved leaves. Serve with Stir-fried Rainbow Vegetables *(page 111)*.

Fried Chicken

10 chicken drumsticks
1 teaspoon tamarind pulp *(see page 38)*
1 whole onion
1 teaspoon ground turmeric or 7.5-cm / 3-inch piece of fresh turmeric *(see page 66)*, peeled and chopped
1 teaspoon salt
½ teaspoon sugar
½ small cup of oil

PREPARATION
Wash the chicken drumsticks and cut several deep slits into the flesh of each drumstick to let heat and flavour in.
Extract the tamarind juice by mixing it with 3 tablespoons of hot water and squeezing. Discard the pulp.
In a food processor or blender, grind the onion.
In a large bowl, mix the tamarind juice, turmeric, salt, sugar and onion well. Toss the chicken in the mixture and leave to marinate for 2 hours or more.

COOKING
Heat the oil in a stainless-steel or non-stick wok or frying pan and shallow-fry the chicken over moderate heat until golden brown.
Serve hot or cold.

Coriander

Also known as *ketumbar* in Southeast Asia, this is one of the world's most popular flavourings. The dried seeds are used as a spice and the fresh leaves as a herb (often called Chinese parsley or cilantro). The seeds have a peppery orangey flavour, while the green herb is quite different in character with a unique flavour that goes particularly well with chillies. Fresh leaf coriander is now quite widely available, but only some better markets and ethnic shops will sell you the stalks with the roots still attached and these are invaluable as a flavouring in dishes like the one above. If you can't buy coriander complete with roots, just get a much bigger bunch and use all the stalks.

Chicken with Hot-and-sour Bite

500 g / 1 lb boneless chicken meat
2 teaspoons cornflour
2 tablespoons soy sauce
1 tablespoon palm sugar *(see page 90)*
2 tablespoons sesame oil
2 tablespoons black rice vinegar *(see page 107)*
2.5-cm / 1-inch piece of ginger, peeled
2 garlic cloves
1 teaspoon whole black peppercorns
30 g / 1 oz dried red chillies
2 tablespoons oil
2 heads of star anise *(see below)*

PREPARATION

Cut the chicken into small cubes.
In a bowl, mix the cornflour, soy sauce, palm sugar, sesame oil
and vinegar. Toss the chicken in this mixture to season it.
Chop the garlic.
Coarsely crush the whole peppercorns.
Chop the red chillies and remove the seeds.

COOKING

Heat the oil in a heavy-based saucepan and fry the chillies,
crushed peppercorns, star anise and garlic until aromatic.
Remove from the pan and set aside.
Add the seasoned chicken to the pan and stir-fry for 10 minutes.
Return the fried spices to the pan and stir-fry for
5 minutes more.

Star Anise

Known as *bunga lawang* in Southeast Asia, this spice
is the nut from a tree related to the magnolia. The
brittle outer pod is in the shape of an eight-
pointed star, hence its name, and it is this
dried pod that is broken up or ground for use
as a flavouring as the seeds inside have a much less
forceful flavour. Now widely available in better food
shops and larger supermarkets, the sweet liquorice-like
anise flavour is also one of the principal elements in
Chinese five-spice powder *(see page 75)*.

Curry Puffs

225 g / 8 oz skinless chicken breast
1 large potato
500 g / 1 lb plain flour
1 egg
2 tablespoons oil
1 onion, chopped
1 tablespoon ground coriander
¼ teaspoon ground turmeric
¼ teaspoon cumin
pinch of fennel seeds, ground
1 teaspoon chilli powder
1 teaspoon salt
oil for deep-frying

PREPARATION

Cut the chicken into 1-cm / ½-inch cubes.
Cook the potato in boiling salted water until just tender. Drain
and leave to cool. Cut the cooked potato into pieces about the
same size as the chicken.
Sieve the flour into a large mixing bowl. Add the egg with
125 ml / 4 fl oz water and the oil. Mix well and then knead until
you have a smooth dough. Let the dough rest in the refrigerator.

COOKING

Heat 2 tablespoons of the oil in a wok or frying pan and fry the
onion until soft. Add the chicken and stir-fry for 10 minutes until
firm and white.
Stir in the spices, followed by the potatoes and salt. Stir-fry over
a low heat for 5 minutes more. Leave to cool.
Divide the rested dough into about 24 small balls. Roll each
ball into a small circle and put 1 tablespoon of the cold
filling on top. Fold the round over to make a semicircle
and press the edge with a fork all round to seal.
Heat oil for deep-frying over moderate heat and fry
the puffs, in batches if necessary, until golden brown.

Chicken and Quails' Eggs

2 skinless chicken breasts
12 quails' eggs
2 tablespoons soy sauce
1½ teaspoons cornflour
1 potato
1 carrot
1 Webb's lettuce
2 garlic cloves
2 tablespoons oil
2 tablespoons rice wine or dry sherry
2 spring onions, chopped, for garnish
2 sprigs of coriander, for garnish

Preparation

Dice the chicken breasts.
Hard-boil the quails' eggs (about 2 minutes), allow to cool and shell.
In a bowl, mix the soy sauce and cornflour. Toss the chicken in the mixture to season.
Dice the potato. Cut the carrot into matchstick strips. Shred the lettuce finely.
Chop the garlic finely.

Cooking

Heat the oil in a wok or frying pan and fry the garlic, chicken and potato for 15 minutes.
Add the quails' eggs, 5 tablespoons of water and the rice wine. Stir well.
Meanwhile, arrange the lettuce and carrot around the edge of a large platter so that the centre is empty.
Pour the contents of the wok or pan into the centre of the platter (keeping back the quails' eggs to scatter over the top) and serve, garnished with spring onions and coriander.

Pineapple Chicken Lemak

1 small chicken, about 1.25 kg / 2½ lb
1 whole pineapple
1 stalk of lemon grass *(see page 48)*
1 red onion
4 candlenuts *(see page 41)*
5-cm / 2-inch piece of fresh turmeric *(see page 66)*, peeled
2 tablespoons oil
1 teaspoon shrimp paste *(blachan, see page 18)*
1 teaspoon salt
1 teaspoon sugar
225 ml / 8 fl oz coconut milk

Preparation

Clean the chicken and remove the skin. Cut the chicken into 16 pieces *(see page 56)*.
Peel the pineapple and cut it into cubes.
Pound the lemon grass.
Grind the red onion, candlenuts and turmeric together to a paste.

Cooking

Heat the oil in a large heavy-based pan and add the lemon grass and the onion mixture with the shrimp paste. Fry until aromatic and a medium light brown colour.
Add the chicken and stir-fry for 5 minutes.
Lastly, add the pineapple, salt, sugar and coconut milk, and simmer for 15 minutes.

Chicken with Black Bean Sauce and Cashew Nuts

2 large skinless chicken breasts
1 teaspoon cornflour
1 tablespoon oyster sauce
1 spring onion
1 garlic clove
1 whole red chilli
2.5-cm / 1-inch piece of ginger, peeled
1 tablespoons oil
1 teaspoon black bean sauce *(see below)*
dash of white wine
½ cup chicken stock or water
handful of cashew nuts, for garnish

PREPARATION

Slice the chicken thinly across the grain.
In a large bowl, mix the cornflour and oyster sauce. Toss the chicken in the mixture and set aside.
Cut the spring onion into 5-cm / 2-inch pieces.
Slice the garlic, chilli and ginger.

COOKING

Heat the oil in a wok or frying pan and add the sliced garlic, ginger and chilli with the black bean sauce. Stir-fry until aromatic.
Add the spring onion and marinated chicken. Stir well and add the wine and stock or water. Continue to stir-fry for a further 5 minutes.
Serve garnished with cashew nuts.

Shocking Chicken Wings

900 g / 2 lb chicken wings
1½ teaspoons salt
2 red chillies
1 onion
4 candlenuts *(see page 41)*
1 garlic clove
½ teaspoon ground turmeric or 1-cm / ½-inch piece of fresh turmeric *(page 66)*, peeled
2 lemons
1 teaspoon sugar
oil for deep-frying

PREPARATION

Wash the chicken wings, pat dry with paper towels and season with 1 teaspoon of salt.
Grind the chillies, onion, candlenuts, garlic and turmeric to a coarse paste.
Squeeze the juice from the lemons.

COOKING

Deep-fry the chicken wings in hot oil until golden brown. Drain well and set aside in a warm place.
In a wok or frying pan, cook the chilli paste over a very low heat for 5 minutes.
Add the sugar, the remaining salt and the lemon juice. Stir-fry for 2 minutes and then pour over the wings.
Toss to coat thoroughly and serve.

Black Bean Sauce

Sold in bottles and cans, this is nothing more than mashed cooked salted and fermented whole soya beans. It may be quite coarsely mashed, so you might want to purée the beans down further yourself. Its strong earthy flavour goes well with meat - especially beef - and fish dishes and is at its best when combined with chillies. Try a little in your next cottage pie to give it a lift.

Chicken with Bamboo Shoots

2 skinless chicken breasts
about 115 g / 4 oz drained canned bamboo shoots
1 large red onion
2.5-cm / 1-inch piece of galangal *(see page 25)*, peeled
1 stalk of lemon grass *(see page 48)*
2.5-cm / 1-inch piece of fresh turmeric *(see page 66)*, peeled
4 candlenuts *(see page 41)*
2 tablespoons oil
¼ teaspoon shrimp paste *(blachan, see page 18)*
1 teaspoon sugar
1½ teaspoons salt
225 ml / 8 fl oz coconut milk
12 red chillies, sliced, for garnish

PREPARATION
Slice the chicken and the bamboo shoots into thin slices.
Grind the onion, galangal, lemon grass, turmeric and candlenuts
finely to a paste.

COOKING
Heat the oil in a wok or frying pan and fry all the ground
flavourings with the shrimp paste over moderate heat for
3 minutes, until aromatic (be patient and careful not to burn it!).
Add ½ a small cup of water and the bamboo shoots. Simmer for
15 minutes.
Add the chicken and continue to simmer for 15 minutes.
Stir in the sugar, salt and coconut milk.
Serve hot, garnished with the chilli slices.

Fresh Turmeric

Also known in Indonesia as
kunjit and *haldi* in
India, turmeric
is one of my
favourite
flavourings. The fresh rhizome has
brown skin and bright orange flesh which has a lovely
peppery taste that hints of oranges and ginger (it's a close
relative). The little fingers that stick out from the main
rhizome have the best flavour. Turmeric is famous for its
cleansing properties. It is a powerful antiseptic - the
Indians even pack the dried powder into wounds.

Spicy Chicken with Basil Leaves

275 g / 10 oz skinless chicken breast
20–30 basil leaves
1 teaspoon cornflour
2 tablespoons fish sauce
1 garlic clove
1 small red onion
2 red chillies
1 stalk of lemon grass *(see page 48)*
2 tablespoons oil
125 ml / 4 fl oz coconut milk
¼ teaspoon black pepper

PREPARATION
Slice the chicken thinly across the grain.
Rinse the basil leaves and pat dry with paper towels.
In a large bowl, mix the cornflour with the fish sauce and toss
the chicken in the mixture.
Finely chop the garlic, onion and chillies.
Cut off stalk end of the lemon grass, peel off the hard outer
layers and finely chop the soft interior. Reserve this and the
whole top end of the stalk.

COOKING
Heat the oil in a wok or frying pan and add the garlic, onion and
chillies. Stir-fry for a minute until aromatic.
Add the chicken and continue to stir-fry until the chicken is
cooked through, about 5 minutes more.
Add the coconut milk, basil leaves, black pepper and chopped
and whole lemon grass. Bring to the boil briefly and serve.

Lemon Chicken

2 pieces of skinless chicken breast
2 tablespoons dry white wine
½ teaspoon salt
1 tablespoon flour
1 tablespoon oil
3 sprigs of coriander, for garnish
1 carrot, for garnish

FOR THE LEMON SAUCE:
2 lemons
1 small garlic clove
2.5-cm / 1-inch piece of ginger, peeled
2 teaspoons cornflour
2 tablespoons oil
2 tablespoons sugar
2 tablespoons light soy sauce
½ teaspoon salt

PREPARATION
Cut the chicken across the grain into strips. Season with the wine and salt and dab it in the flour.
Squeeze the juice from the lemons for the sauce. Chop the garlic and ginger.
In a small bowl, mix the cornflour with ½ small cup of water.
Cut the carrot into matchstick shreds.

COOKING
Heat the oil in a wok or frying pan and shallow-fry the chicken over a moderate heat until golden brown. Remove from the pan and transfer to a serving plate.
Make the sauce: heat the oil in a wok or frying pan and stir-fry the garlic and ginger for 1 minute. Then add the lemon juice, sugar, soy sauce, salt and cornflour mixture to thicken.
Pour the sauce over the chicken and garnish with the fresh coriander and carrot shreds.

Chicken with Lime Sauce

500 g / 1 lb skinless chicken breast
1 tablespoon cornflour
2 tablespoons soy sauce
1 teaspoon pepper
2 tablespoons oil

FOR THE LIME SAUCE:
2 whole limes
1 teaspoon cornflour
2 tablespoons oil
1 garlic clove
2 thin slices of ginger
1 tablespoon sugar
1 teaspoon salt
6–7 sprigs of coriander

PREPARATION
Cut the chicken into bite-sized pieces.
In a large bowl, mix the 1 tablespoon of cornflour with the soy sauce and pepper.
Add the pieces of chicken and toss in the mixture to coat well.
Squeeze the lime juice for the sauce into a small bowl, add the 1 teaspoon of cornflour and mix well.
Chop the garlic and coriander.

COOKING
Heat the oil in a wok or frying pan and stir-fry the chicken until golden brown.
While it is cooking, make the sauce: heat the oil in a wok or frying pan and fry the garlic and the ginger for 1 minute.
Add the browned chicken with the lime juice mixture, sugar, salt and coriander. Stir-fry for 2 minutes, then add ½ a small cup of water and simmer for 5 minutes.
Serve hot with plain boiled rice.

Steamed Chicken in Red Wine

1 small chicken, about 1.25 kg / 2½ lb
2 teaspoons salt
5-cm / 2-inch piece of ginger, peeled and cut into matchstick shreds
1 cup of red wine
2 spring onions, chopped, for garnish
2 sprigs of coriander, chopped, for garnish

PREPARATION

Clean the chicken and remove the skin and any excess fat.
Rub 1 teaspoon of salt all over the chicken and then rinse off.
Cut the chicken into 10-14 pieces *(see page 56)*. Cut deep slits on all the pieces to let heat and flavour into the flesh. Sprinkle the remaining salt and the ginger over the chicken pieces.

COOKING

Steam the chicken in a bamboo steamer over a high heat for 20 minutes.
Add the red wine and steam for a further 5 minutes. Turn off the heat but leave the steamer covered for another 5 minutes.
Remove the chicken from the steamer, transfer to a plate and garnish with spring onions and coriander.
Serve hot.

Dry Chicken Curry

1 small chicken, about 1.25 kg / 2½ lb
3 large red onions
4 candlenuts *(see page 41)*
2 tablespoons oil
2 teaspoons chilli powder
1 teaspoon sugar
2 teaspoons salt
225 ml / 8 fl oz coconut milk

PREPARATION

Clean the chicken and cut it into 10 pieces *(see page 56)*, leaving the skin on.
Chop the red onions.
Pound the candlenuts.

COOKING

Heat the oil in a wok or frying pan and fry the onions and candlenuts until lightly browned.
Add the chicken and chilli powder and continue to fry until the chicken is lightly browned.
Add ½ a small cup of water with the sugar and salt, and fry for 5 minutes more.
Then lower the heat and add the coconut milk. Cook gently until the curry is dry.

Chicken on Toast

300 g / 10½ oz skinless chicken breast
2 garlic cloves
1 egg
1½ teaspoons cornflour
2 teaspoons fish sauce
1 tablespoon oyster sauce
dash of dry white wine
½ teaspoon black pepper
6 slices of thinly sliced white bread, crusts removed
2 tablespoons sesame seeds
2 cups of oil

PREPARATION
In a food processor or with two knives, mince the chicken and garlic finely and mix with the egg, cornflour, fish sauce, oyster sauce, white wine and pepper.
With a spatula, spread the chicken paste on the bread. Sprinkle with the sesame seeds and press them into the mixture.

COOKING
Heat the oil in a wok or frying pan and fry the bread slices, paste-side down, until golden. Drain on piles of paper towels.

Mummy Saucy Chicken

This dish is so-called because it and stir-fried vegetables were the only things that my mother ever cooked for us, when she wasn't gambling.

1 small chicken, about 1.25 kg / 2½ lb
1½ teaspoons salt
2–3 tablespoons soy sauce
1 teaspoon black pepper
4 whole limes
6 red chillies
½ small cup of oil
4 tablespoons sugar

PREPARATION
Cut the chicken into 20 pieces *(see page 56)*, keeping the skin on. In a large bowl, mix ½ teaspoon of the salt, the soy sauce and black pepper. Toss the chicken pieces in the mixture and leave to marinate for 2 hours or more.
Squeeze the juice from the limes.
Pound the red chillies

COOKING
Heat the oil in a frying pan and fry the chicken pieces until golden brown all over. It should take about 15 minutes. Remove from the pan and transfer to a serving plate.
Mix the pounded chillies with the lime juice, remaining salt and the sugar. Pour this on top of the cooked chicken and serve.

Oyster Sauce

This classic bottled Chinese sauce made from puréed oysters is deep in colour and rich in flavour. Strangely, it is more often used to strengthen the flavour of meat and vegetable dishes than those made with fish and other seafood. Nowadays it is available from most good supermarkets and it keeps well for months in the refrigerator. Use it to perk up any vegetable stir-fry.

Five-spice Flavoured Deep-fried Chicken with Ginger Dip

1 chicken, about 1.25 kg / 2½ lb
1 teaspoon five-spice powder *(see opposite)*
½ teaspoon pepper
½ teaspoon sugar
3 tablespoons soy sauce
oil for deep-frying

FOR THE GINGER DIP:
100 g / 3½ oz peeled ginger
2 teaspoons salt
3 tablespoons oil
1 tablespoon sesame oil

PREPARATION

Cut the chicken into 8 pieces *(see page 56)*.
Mix the five-spice powder, pepper, sugar and soy sauce. Season the chicken pieces with the mixture and leave to marinate for 2 hours or more.
Make the ginger dip: in a food processor or blender, grind the ginger fairly finely. Add the salt and both oils. Process briefly to mix well and pour into a serving bowl.

COOKING

Deep-fry the chicken in 2 or 3 batches over a moderate heat until well browned. Drain on paper towels as they are cooked.
Serve hot or cold, with the ginger dip.

Chicken Salad with Five-spice

350 g / 12 oz chicken breast
115 g / 4 oz cucumber
115 g / 4 oz carrots
115 g / 4 oz white radish *(mooli, see below)*
115 g/ 4 oz white cabbage
2 limes
2 tablespoons sesame seeds
½ teaspoon salt
1 tablespoon sugar
1 tablespoon sesame oil
1 teaspoon five-spice powder *(see opposite)*
2 tablespoons oil

PREPARATION

Slice the chicken very thinly across the grain.
Slice the cucumber, carrots and radish into matchstick strips and place them in a large salad bowl. Shred the cabbage and add to the bowl.
In a small bowl, mix together the juice from the 2 limes, the sesame seeds, salt, sugar and sesame oil and add in the five-spice powder.

COOKING

Heat the oil in a wok or frying pan and stir-fry the chicken until just cooked through (the pieces are firm and opaque, with no pink juices). Remove and set aside.
Pour the dressing in the small bowl over the vegetables and toss thoroughly.
Pile the chicken on top to serve.

Mooli

Also known as daikon or China rose, this large pale-coloured radish looks more like a big smooth parsnip and has a wonderful sharp peppery flavour. Buy only firm moolis that seem heavy for their size (they're in many good supermarkets now). They keep well in the refrigerator for some time, so don't worry about buying one that is bigger than you need for one dish.

Chicken with Ginger and Oyster Sauce

400 g / 14 oz skinless chicken breast
7.5-cm / 3-inch piece of ginger, peeled
2 tablespoons oil
1½ teaspoons cornflour
125 ml / 4 fl oz chicken stock *(see page 19)*
2 tablespoons oyster sauce
3 tablespoons dry white wine

PREPARATION

Cut the chicken across the grain into slices about 1 cm / ½ inch thick.
Slice the ginger into matchstick strips.

COOKING

Heat the oil in a wok or frying pan and stir-fry the ginger until aromatic.
Add the chicken and stir-fry about for 10 minutes.
Add the cornflour and keep on stirring for a minute or so.
Stir in the stock and the oyster sauce.
Lastly stir in the wine over a highish heat and serve.

Stewed Duck with Five-spice Powder

1 whole duck, about 2.25 kg / 5 lb
1 tablespoon five-spice powder *(see below)*
1 teaspoon salt
4 garlic cloves
7.5-cm / 3-inch piece of galangal *(see page 25)*, peeled
6 tablespoons ketjap manis *(see page 92)*
3 tablespoons dark brown sugar

PREPARATION

Wash the duck and trim off as much fat as possible.
Rub the five-spice powder and salt all over the duck.
Crush the garlic and galangal.

COOKING

Place the whole duck in a large pot with no water and place over a moderate heat.
Turn the duck on all sides until it is well browned all over.
Add the galangal and garlic, followed by 4 small cups of water, the ketjap manis and the sugar. Bring to the boil, then lower the heat to moderate and cook for 1½ hours to reduce the liquid to a thick sauce.
Remove the duck and carve. Serve with the sauce and plain boiled rice.

Chinese Five-spice Powder

This mixture of ground spices consists of roughly equal parts star anise, Sichuan (or anise) pepper, cassia or cinnamon, fennel seeds and cloves. It is very popular as a flavouring for meat and poultry but, as it is so powerful, use it cautiously.

Pork – you pine?

Meat Dishes

4

As you can imagine, generally meat is a bit of a luxury in the East and is treated as such. It is used much more as another flavouring ingredient rather than the core of the meal, as in the old-fashioned (but still all-too-prevalent) 'meat and two veg' attitude here. To make it go further it is either cut into bite-sized cubes or sliced thinly (across the grain for maximum tenderness). As you are not using all that much of it in the recipes that follow you can afford to go for the best-quality lean fillet or tenderloin of beef or pork and lamb leg steaks. Such lean tender meat best suits the rapid cooking of stir-frying. On the other side of the coin, pork spare ribs still represent one of the best bargains at the butchers and everyone loves them!

'Brambly Apples' Stuffed with Pork and Mushrooms

This dish is very versatile – it makes a lovely starter, or serve it with Stir-fried Rainbow Vegetables *(page 111)* and Fried Rice with Nuts *(page 124)* for an unusual Sunday lunch.

4 medium to large Bramley apples
60 g / 2 oz dried mushrooms
175 g / 6 oz lean minced pork
60 g / 2 oz carrots
2 spring onions
2 sprigs of coriander
1 tablespoon light soy sauce
1 tablespoon fish sauce
1 teaspoon black pepper
1½ teaspoons cornflour

PREPARATION

Wash the apples and cut out the centre of the flesh with a small sharp knife, leaving about 1 cm / ½ inch of flesh around the edges.
Put the mushrooms in a bowl and pour boiling water over them to cover. Leave to soak for 5 minutes, then drain.
Mince the pork if not ready-prepared.
Chop the removed flesh of one of the apples, the mushrooms, carrots, spring onions and coriander. In a bowl, mix all of these with the pork, soy sauce, fish sauce, pepper and cornflour.

COOKING

Stuff the filling mixture into the apples and steam for 20 minutes over a high heat in a bamboo steamer.
Serve immediately.

Fish Sauce

Various types of fish sauce are used all over Southeast Asia, all made much the same way from fermented salted fish. The Thai version is called *nam pla*, the Vietnamese *nuoc nam*, and the Burmese *ngapi*. Although made from rotting fish, they don't have an overpowering aroma or flavour, and don't impart a fishy taste to cooked dishes, giving an effect more like salty soy sauces. They do, however, add a special depth of flavour that is essential to some dishes. As with the very similar *blachan* pastes, if you can't get any fish sauce then a little anchovy essence or paste will give you some of the effect.

Babi Satay with Pineapple Sauce

275 g / 10 oz lean pork
1 stalk of lemon grass *(see page 48)*
1 small onion
½ teaspoon ground cumin
¾ teaspoon ground turmeric
¾ teaspoon salt
1 tablespoon sugar
1 tablespoon oil
12 satay sticks, about 10–15 cm / 4–6 inches long

FOR THE PINEAPPLE SAUCE:
1 small can of crushed pineapple in juice
1 tablespoon sugar

PREPARATION

Slice the pork thinly across the grain (about 5 mm / ¼ inch thick) and place in a large mixing bowl.
In a food processor, grind the lemon grass and onion and add to the bowl.
Add the cumin, turmeric, salt, sugar and oil. Mix well so that the pork is evenly coated and leave to marinate for at least 1 hour.
Thread the marinated pork pieces on the satay sticks.

COOKING

First make the pineapple sauce: in small pan, boil the pineapple with the sugar and a pinch of salt for about 10 minutes.
Grill or barbecue the satays on both sides over a high heat, but take care not to overcook (stop while the pork is still moist and juicy).
Serve the pork satays with the pineapple sauce.

Boiled Spicy Pork

1.75 kg / 4 lb leg of pork
3 tablespoons dark brown sugar
2 teaspoons salt, or to taste
2 tablespoons ground coriander
5 tablespoons soy sauce
1 teaspoon black pepper
2 teaspoons garlic powder
1 large onion
4 tablespoons cooking oil

PREPARATION

Rinse the pork and pat dry with paper towels.
In a large bowl, mix the sugar, salt, coriander, soy sauce, pepper and garlic powder. Season the pork with this mixture and leave to marinate for 2 hours or more. Turn the meat a few times.
Chop the onion.

COOKING

Heat the oil in a large casserole and fry the onion until lightly browned.
Then add the pork and turn it around a few times in order to brown the meat on all sides.
Add 3 small cups of water and bring to the boil. Cover and simmer for 45 minutes.
Uncover, turn the heat to high and boil rapidly for about 30 minutes to reduce the sauce.
Remove the meat and cut it into slices.
Serve with the reduced sauce.

Soy Sauce

This is the most widely used of the range of salted, fermented soya bean products found all over the Far East. There are many types from all nations, but the two main varieties are light soy sauce and dark soy sauce, light being more salty and dark sweeter (but still fairly salty). Indeed soy sauce is used at the table in the way that salt is in the West. A vast range of soy sauces is now widely available almost everywhere; so try a few until you find one that suits your taste. A good soy sauce can perk up almost any savoury dish (try it in your Bolognese), and if you haven't got any stock when it is called for, just use water with a tablespoon or two of good soy sauce stirred into it.

Sweet-and-sour Pork

275 g / 10 oz lean pork
3 heaped tablespoons self-raising flour
pinch of salt
oil for deep-frying

FOR THE SWEET-AND-SOUR SAUCE:
1 tablespoon oil
½ onion
1 garlic clove
5-cm / 2-inch piece of ginger, peeled
2 tablespoons white wine vinegar
2 tablespoons tomato ketchup
2 tablespoons sugar
1 tablespoon cornflour
2 teaspoons salt, or to taste

PREPARATION

Cut the pork into bite-sized cubes.
Whisk the flour and salt together with ½ small cup of water to make a smooth batter.
Chop the onion, garlic and ginger for the sauce.

COOKING

First make the sweet-and-sour sauce: heat the oil in a wok or frying pan (preferably stainless steel or non-stick) until fairly hot and stir-fry the onion, garlic and ginger until aromatic.
Add the vinegar, ketchup and sugar with ½ cup of water and bring to the boil.
Stir in the cornflour and the salt and keep stirring until the sauce is thick and smooth.
Heat the oil for deep-frying. Dip the pieces of pork in the batter and deep-fry until golden brown. Drain well.
Pour the sauce over the pork to serve.

Sesame Chilli Pork

275 g / 10 oz lean pork fillet
2–3 tablespoons soy sauce
2 teaspoons cornflour
2 garlic cloves
2 spring onions
2 dried chillies
2 tablespoons oil
1 tablespoon sesame paste *(tahini or seeds ground to a paste)*
1 tablespoon sesame oil
1 teaspoon sugar
1 tablespoon Worcestershire sauce

PREPARATION

Cut the pork into thin slices across the grain.
Mix the soy sauce and cornflour. Season the pork with this mixture.
Chop the garlic and the spring onions. Slice the chillies.

COOKING

Heat the oil in a wok or frying pan and stir-fry the chopped garlic and spring onions until aromatic.
Add the chillies and the sesame paste and stir-fry for 1 minute.
Add the sliced pork and continue to stir-fry for a further 5 minutes over high heat.
Add the sesame oil, sugar and Worcestershire sauce and stir-fry for 2 minutes more.
Serve hot with plain white rice.

Babi Taucheo Bedas
Pork with Yellow Bean Sauce

1.5 kg / 3¼ lb lean belly pork with skin
1 chilli
1 large onion
5 garlic cloves
2–3 spring onions, for garnish
2 tablespoons oil
2 tablespoons crushed yellow bean sauce *(see page 118)*
4 tablespoons dark soy sauce
1 lump of rock sugar *(see page 140)*
3 small cups of stock or water

PREPARATION

Cut the pork into 3.5-cm / 1½-inch chunks with the skin.
Slice the chilli, onion and garlic,
Chop the spring onions.

COOKING

Heat the oil in a heavy-based pan and stir-fry the garlic until lightly browned.
Add the onion and yellow bean sauce and stir-fry for a few minutes.
Add the pork with the soy sauce, rock sugar, the chilli and stock or water. Stir well, bring to a simmer and cover.
Leave to simmer until the pork is cooked and the sauce is reduced to a thick gravy, 30-45 minutes.
Serve hot, garnished with the spring onions.

Sesame Oil

Oriental sesame oil is extracted from sesame seeds that have first been roasted (look for oil with a rich golden brown colour) giving a much more powerful nutty flavour. Rather than for cooking (it breaks down easily), it is mostly used as a dressing, especially on vegetables, a few drops being dribbled over the dish off the heat just before serving. Be careful not to use too much as it can drown other flavours. Try a little on your Brussels sprouts next time you are having them with lamb.

Straits Chinese Pork Satay

500 g / 1 lb lean pork fillet
4 dried chillies
2 large onions
8 candlenuts *(see page 41)*
1 pinch of shrimp paste *(blachan, see page 18)*
5-cm / 2-inch piece of lemon grass *(see page 48)*
225 ml / 8 fl oz coconut milk
3 eggs, lightly beaten
salt to taste
sugar to taste

PREPARATION

Slice the pork thinly across the grain and put in a large pan.
Pound or finely grind together the chillies, onions, candlenuts, shrimp paste and lemon grass.
Mix these with the pork and add the coconut milk.

COOKING

Bring to the boil, lower the heat and simmer for 45 minutes.
Add in the beaten eggs and stir until cooked, 2-3 minutes. Add sugar and salt to taste.
Serve hot with plain boiled rice.

Stewed Chinese Pork Chops

4 pork chops
1 teaspoon black pepper
1 tablespoon soy sauce
1 teaspoon cornflour
1 onion
1 red chilli
4 small potatoes
4 tomatoes
2 tablespoons oil
4 tablespoons tomato ketchup
2 tablespoons sugar, or to taste
2 teaspoons salt, or to taste
115 g / 4 oz shelled garden peas

PREPARATION

Bash the pork chops to flatten and tenderize them.
Mix the pepper, soy sauce and cornflour and season the chops with this mixture.
Slice the onion and separate the slices into rings.
Slice the chilli.
Cut the potatoes into wedges
Cut the tomatoes into quarters.

COOKING

Heat the oil in a frying pan and fry the pork chops for 5 minutes on each side to brown them lightly and set aside.
Add the potatoes to the pan and fry them until golden brown and set aside.
Discard all but about 2 tablespoons of the fat in the pan and fry the onion rings and chilli for 2 minutes.
Return the pork chops to the pan together with 1 small cup of water, the tomatoes, ketchup, sugar and salt. Bring to the boil, lower the heat and simmer for 10 minutes.
Add the peas and potatoes and cook for a further 2 minutes.
Serve hot.

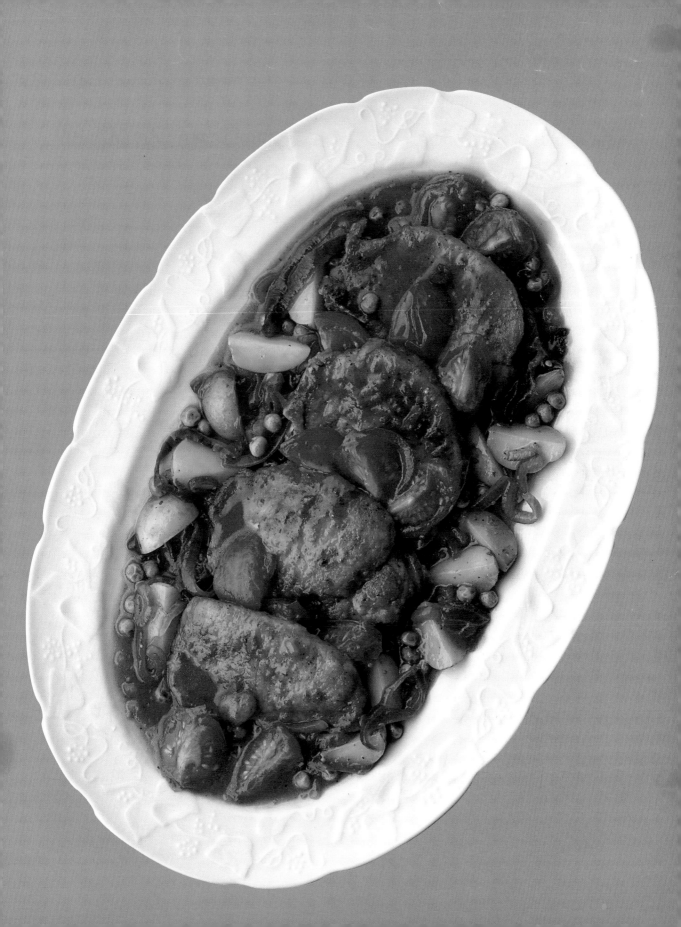

Nancy's Favourite Spare Ribs

1 kg / 2 lb pork spare ribs
4 garlic cloves
2 chillies
2 teaspoons maple syrup
3 tablespoons soy sauce
2 tablespoons tomato ketchup
1 teaspoon chilli powder
2 tablespoons brown sugar
1 teaspoon pepper
1 tablespoons sesame seeds, for garnish

PREPARATION

Trim off excess fat from the ribs and put the trimmed ribs in a large bowl.
Crush the garlic and chillies and add these, together with all the remaining ingredients except the sesame seeds, to the bowl. Mix well with your hand or a wooden spatula and leave to marinate for a minimum of 2 hours, but preferably overnight (refrigerated, of course).

COOKING

Put all the contents of the bowl in a large pan and add just enough water to cover the pork. Bring to the boil and simmer the marinated pork for half an hour.
Preheat a barbecue, grill or griddle and drain the spare ribs, reserving the now reduced and rich cooking liquid. Put the spare ribs to cook and brown them nicely on both sides.
Serve hot, sprinkled with the sesame seeds, and pour the reserved gravy on top.

Steamed Spare Ribs with Hot Sauce

500 g / 1 lb pork spare ribs
2 thin slices of ginger
2 garlic cloves
1 red chilli
½ teaspoon salt
1 teaspoon sesame oil
1½ tablespoons black bean sauce *(see page 64)*
1 teaspoon sugar
2 tablespoons hoisin sauce *(see below)*
2 tablespoons rice wine or dry sherry
2 teaspoons cornflour

PREPARATION

Remove as much fat as possible from the spare ribs and cut the ribs into 5-cm / 2-inch segments.
In a food processor or blender, grind the ginger, garlic and chilli.
In a large pan of boiling salted water, boil the spare ribs for 20 minutes. Drain.
In a large bowl, mix the spare ribs with the blended ginger mixture, together with the sesame oil, black bean sauce, sugar, hoisin sauce, rice wine or sherry and cornflour. Mix well and leave to marinate for 2 hours or more in the refrigerator.

COOKING

Steam in a bamboo steamer for about 1 hour.
Serve hot.

Hoisin Sauce

Often called Chinese barbecue sauce, this rich thick sauce is made from puréed soy beans, flavoured with sugar, salt, chillies, vinegar and sesame oil. Its almost fruity flavour is particularly suited to meat dishes. It is available from most large supermarkets.

Beef Noodles in Black Bean Sauce

400 g / 14 oz beef fillet
1 teaspoon cornflour
2 tablespoons oyster sauce
2 garlic cloves
2.5-cm / 1-inch piece of ginger, peeled
1 whole chilli
1 teaspoon black bean sauce *(see page 64)*
2 tablespoons oil
500 g / 1 lb fresh flat rice noodles

PREPARATION
Slice the beef fillet thinly across the grain.
In a large bowl, mix the cornflour and oyster sauce, add the beef strips and toss to mix well.
Chop the garlic, ginger and chilli.

COOKING
Heat the oil in a wok or frying pan and stir-fry the noodles until lightly browned. Remove and set aside on a plate.
Stir-fry the garlic, ginger, chilli and black bean sauce quickly for 1 minute.
Return the noodles to the pan and stir-fry until piping hot.
Serve.

Beef and Green Pepper

500 g / 1 lb lean steak
1 large green pepper
2 garlic cloves
2.5-cm / 1-inch piece of ginger, peeled
1 teaspoon pepper
1½ teaspoons cornflour
3 tablespoons soy sauce
2 tablespoons oil
4 tablespoons dry sherry

PREPARATION
Slice the steak across the grain.
Slice the green pepper into strips.
Chop the garlic and slice the ginger into matchstick strips.
In a bowl, mix the pepper, cornflour and soy sauce. Toss the steak in this mixture to season it.

COOKING
Heat a tablespoon of oil in a wok or frying pan and quickly stir-fry the green pepper. Remove and transfer to a plate.
Heat the remaining oil and stir-fry the garlic and ginger briefly until aromatic.
Turn the heat up to high, add the seasoned steak and stir-fry for 5 minutes.
Add the sherry and 4 tablespoons of water and stir quickly.
Lastly add in the green pepper, stir-fry for 30 seconds and serve.

Beef with Mango

250 g / 9 oz lean beef fillet
2 tablespoons oyster sauce
1 teaspoon cornflour
½ teaspoon pepper
1½ teaspoons brown sugar
2 garlic cloves
1 whole ripe mango
4 sprigs of coriander, for garnish
2 spring onions, for garnish
2 tablespoons oil
4 thin slices of ginger
4 tablespoons white wine

PREPARATION

Slice the beef thinly across the grain.
In a large bowl, mix the oyster sauce, cornflour, black pepper and
sugar. Toss the beef in this mixture to season it.
Chop the garlic.
Peel the mango and slice the flesh thinly *(see page 142)*.
Chop the coriander and spring onions for garnish.

COOKING

Heat the oil in a wok or frying pan and stir-fry the garlic and
ginger until aromatic.
Increase the heat to high, add the beef and stir-fry for 5 minutes.
Stir in the wine and the mango to warm it through.
Garnish with the chopped coriander and spring onions.

Party Beef

This dish is great for parties as it makes lots with very little
effort and at relatively little cost.

1 kg / 2 lb stewing beef
4 red onions
4 red chillies
4 garlic cloves
2.5-cm / 1-inch piece of ginger, peeled
5-cm / 2-inch piece of fresh turmeric *(see page 66)*, peeled
1 tablespoon coriander seeds
1 teaspoon cumin seeds
1 teaspoon fennel seeds
3 tablespoons oil
225 ml / 8 fl oz canned coconut milk

PREPARATION

Trim off all the fat from the beef and cut the beef into cubes.
Chop the onions finely.
In a food processor, coarsely grind the chillies, garlic, ginger and
turmeric with the coriander, cumin and fennel seeds.

COOKING

Heat the oil in a wok or frying pan and stir-fry the onion for
1 minute. Add all the ground ingredients and continue to stir-fry
for 5 minutes more.
Over moderate heat, add the beef and stir occasionally for
4 minutes until you can smell its aroma.
Add a small cup of water with the coconut milk and boil for
5 minutes, then lower the heat and simmer for 1 hour until the
beef is tender.
Serve with plain boiled rice.

Makes a
party go with
a swing!

Nancy's Beef Curry

1 kg / 2 lb rump or stewing steak
2 large red onions
2 garlic cloves
2.5-cm / 1-inch piece of ginger, peeled
2 tablespoons oil
2 tablespoons tomato purée
1 teaspoon ground cumin
2 tablespoons curry powder
1 teaspoon salt
1½ teaspoons brown sugar

PREPARATION

Cut the steak across the grain into 2.5-cm / 1-inch cubes.
Finely chop the onions, garlic and ginger.

COOKING

Heat the oil in a large heavy-based pan and fry the onion, garlic and ginger until lightly browned.
Add the steak, tomato purée, cumin, curry powder, salt and sugar, and continue to stir-fry until aromatic.
Add ½ a small cup of water and bring to the boil. Lower the heat and simmer for 30 minutes, or until the meat is tender. The result should be a semi-dry curry.
Serve hot with plain boiled rice.

Beef Salad

225 g / 8 oz lean beef fillet
½ teaspoon salt
½ teaspoon black pepper
5 tablespoons sesame seeds,
preferably a mix of black and white
1 chilli
2 sprigs of coriander
1 spring onion
2 sprigs of basil leaves
2 tablespoons oil
2 tablespoons fish sauce
2 tablespoons sesame oil
2 tablespoons black rice vinegar
2 tablespoons palm sugar *(see below)*
1 bag of mixed ready-prepared salad leaves

PREPARATION

Slice the beef thinly across the grain and pound the slices to flatten and tenderize them. Season with salt and pepper and leave for 10 minutes.
Toss the beef in the sesame seeds, coating it well.
Slice the chilli, coriander, spring onion and basil.

COOKING

Heat the oil in a wok or frying pan and brown the slices of beef on both sides, a few at a time. Transfer to a plate.
Mix the fish sauce with the sesame oil, vinegar, sugar and the chopped chilli, coriander, spring onion and basil.
Arrange the salad leaves on a serving plate, pour the mixed sauce around them and pile the beef in the middle to serve.

Palm Sugar

Various types of palm sugar, made from either the sugar palm or the coconut palm, are sold in most Oriental shops under the general term *gula mérah* (red sugar). Usually in the form of a very hard block, you have to chop, scrape or grate off what you need. Palm sugar has an unusual and distinctive caramel flavour, but an unrefined dark brown sugar can be used instead if you can't find it.

Barbecue Beef

900 g / 2 lb sirloin or rump steak
3 tablespoons ketjap manis *(see below)*
2 tablespoons brown sugar
1 teaspoon black pepper
2 tablespoons oil

COOKING

Slice the steak thinly across the grain.
In a large bowl, mix the sugar, ketjap manis, black pepper and oil.
Toss the steak in this mixture to season it. Leave to marinate for up to 2 hours.

COOKING

Barbecue or grill the steak until done to taste.
Serve with salad or noodles.

Beef with Ginger and Brandy

For great dramatic effect, make 'sizzling beef' by finishing this dish off on a preheated sizzling plate at the table.

400 g / 14 oz fillet steak
4 tablespoons brandy
1½ teaspoons cornflour
5-cm / 2-inch piece of ginger, peeled
2 spring onions, for garnish
2 sprigs of coriander, for garnish
2 tablespoons oil
1½ tablespoons oyster sauce
3 tablespoons dry white wine

PREPARATION

Slice the steak across the grain and season it with the brandy and cornflour. Leave to marinate while you prepare the other ingredients.
Slice the ginger into matchstick strips.
Chop the spring onions and coriander.

COOKING

Heat the oil in a wok or frying pan and stir-fry the ginger until aromatic.
Add the steak and stir-fry for 5 minutes over high heat.
Stir in the oyster sauce.
Sprinkle in 3 tablespoons of water and stir.
Lastly stir in the wine and serve garnished with the spring onions and coriander.

Ketjap Manis

This is a thick sweet version of soy sauce from Indonesia that probably gave us the word 'ketchup'. If you can't find it, sweeten some soy sauce with a spoonful or two of palm sugar or brown sugar.

Ben's Guide to Good Grilling

1 The best way of getting the effect of a barbecue or really hot grill in your kitchen is to use a ridged grilling pan or griddle. These are made of cast iron so they absorb lots of heat and can then really scar the food (but they are not very expensive!).

2 If you want (and especially if you're grilling over coals or naked flames), soak your satay sticks in water before skewering them with food and this will keep the sticks from charring during cooking.

3 Get the barbecue, grill or griddle really good and hot before you start cooking.

4 Don't bother oiling the griddle, there will probably be enough fat in the food or its marinade.

5 So that everything gets cooked at the same rate try to make the pieces to be cooked roughly the same size (especially on satays!)

6 Once you put the food down on the griddle don't be tempted to keep moving it about – leave it to get nice and seared on the underside before you turn it over.

7 To get that nice cross-hatched effect on the surface of the food, turn it over twice, the second time turning it by 45 degrees as well as over so that the second set of sear marks on each side are at right angles to the first.

8 Don't let the food get too scorched or it will just taste bitter.

Sweet Soy Sauce Beef with Chilli

350 g / 12 oz rump steak
1 chilli
7.5-cm / 3-inch piece of ginger, peeled
2 spring onions
2–3 sprigs of coriander
2 tablespoons oil
2 tablespoons ketjap manis *(see page 92)*
½ teaspoon black pepper
1 teaspoon sugar
2 tablespoons oyster sauce
1½ tablespoons cornflour
handful of cashew nuts

PREPARATION
Slice the steak very thinly across the grain.
Slice the chilli, ginger and spring onions.
Chop the coriander.

COOKING
Heat the oil in a wok or frying pan and fry the ginger until
aromatic.
Add the steak and stir well.
Add the chilli, ketjap manis, black pepper, sugar, oyster sauce
and cornflour. Stir-fry for 5 minutes.
Serve garnished with cashew nuts and coriander.

Ginger and Chilli Lamb

250 g / 9 oz lean lamb fillet
2 tablespoons soy sauce
2 teaspoons cornflour
2 dried chillies
1 large fresh red chilli
3 thin slices of ginger
2 spring onions
2 tablespoons oil
1 tablespoon hoisin sauce
½ teaspoon brown sugar
2 tablespoons Chinese black rice vinegar *(see page 107)*

PREPARATION
Slice the lamb thinly across the grain and season the strips with
the soy sauce and cornflour.
Chop the fresh and dried chillies.
Slice the ginger and spring onions into matchstick shreds.

COOKING
Heat the oil in a wok or frying pan and stir-fry the chillies and
ginger until aromatic. Remove and set aside.
Heat the remaining oil, add the hoisin sauce and the lamb and
turn the heat to high. Stir-fry for 5 minutes.
Sprinkle in the reserved chilli and ginger mixture with
4 tablespoons of water, the sugar and vinegar.
Stir-fry briefly over a high heat and serve.

Mushroom Lamb with Chilli

500 g / 1 lb lean lamb fillet
100 g / 3½ oz dried mushrooms
2 green chillies
2 red chillies
1 red onion
2 garlic cloves
4 tablespoons red wine
2 teaspoons cornflour
2 tablespoons soy sauce
1 tablespoon oyster sauce
½ teaspoon black pepper
½ teaspoon brown sugar
2 tablespoons oil

PREPARATION

Slice the lamb thinly across the grain.
Soak the mushrooms in hot water for 10 minutes, then cut off and discard the hard stems and slice the mushrooms thinly.
Slice the chillies, onion and garlic thinly.
Mix together the wine, cornflour, soy sauce, oyster sauce, pepper and sugar.

COOKING

Heat 1 tablespoon of oil in a wok or frying pan and stir-fry the mushrooms, onion and chillies for 3-4 minutes until softened. Remove and set aside.
Heat the remaining oil and stir-fry the garlic and lamb quickly over a high heat until the lamb is well browned.
Add the cornflour mixture and stir well.
Lastly pour over the mushroom mixture and serve.

Potato Happy Ball

175 g / 6 oz lean minced lamb
3 large potatoes
1 medium onion
5 sprigs of coriander
2 tablespoons oil, plus more for shallow-frying the balls
½ teaspoon salt
½ teaspoon ground coriander
½ teaspoon pepper
1 egg, beaten

PREPARATION

Mince the lamb if not ready-prepared.
Peel and quarter the potatoes.
Chop the onion and fresh coriander.

COOKING

Cook the potatoes in a pan of boiling salted water until just tender. Drain and leave to cool, then mash them.
Heat the oil in a wok or frying pan and stir-fry the onion for 1 minute.
Add the minced lamb, salt, ground coriander and the pepper. Stir-fry for 10 minutes.
Remove and transfer to a bowl. Add the chopped coriander and mix well.
Scoop up a tablespoonful of mashed potato in the palm of the hand and flatten it.
Put a spoonful of the filling in the middle and roll the potato up around it, making a ball that totally encloses the filling.
Coat the balls with the egg and shallow-fry till golden brown all over.
Serve hot or cold.

Lamb and Aubergine Curry

1 lean leg of lamb, about 1.25 kg / 2¾ lb
5-cm / 2-inch piece of ginger
4 garlic cloves
2 large onions
3 sprigs of coriander, for garnish
1½ tablespoons oil
1½ tablespoons curry powder
2 teaspoons salt, or to taste
1 teaspoon sugar
275 g / 10 oz aubergine

PREPARATION
Cut the lamb into cubes, trimming off any excess fat.
Grind the ginger and the garlic.
Slice the onions and chop the coriander.

COOKING
Heat the oil in a wok or frying pan and stir-fry the onions until light brown.
Add the ginger and garlic and stir-fry for a few seconds until aromatic.
Add the lamb and continue to stir-fry over a moderate heat until the juices of the meat run.
Add the curry powder and continue to stir-fry briefly.
Add 2 small cups of water, together with the salt and sugar.
Leave to simmer for about 45 minutes or until the meat is tender.
About 10 minutes before the meat is due to be cooked, cut the aubergine into bite-sized chunks and stir them in.
Serve garnished with the coriander.

Lamb Curry

1 lean leg of lamb, about 1.25 kg / 2¾ lb
2 large onions
5-cm / 2-inch piece of ginger, peeled
4 garlic cloves
1½ tablespoons curry powder
1 teaspoon sugar
2 teaspoons salt, or to taste
3 sprigs of coriander
1½ tablespoons oil

PREPARATION
Cut the lamb into cubes, trimming off any excess fat.
Slice the onions.
Grind the ginger and the garlic.
In a large bowl, mix the ginger and garlic with the curry powder, sugar and salt. Toss the lamb in this mixture and leave to marinate for 3 hours or more.
Chop the coriander.

COOKING
Heat the oil in a wok or frying pan and stir-fry the sliced onion until lightly browned.
Add the lamb and continue to stir-fry over moderate heat until the juices of the meat run.
Add 2 small cups of water, bring to the boil and then lower the heat and leave to simmer for about 45 minutes, or until the lamb is tender.
Stir in the coriander and serve.

18-carrot gold!

Vegetable Dishes

The dishes in this chapter vary from simple side dishes to complex vegetable-based main dishes. Although none feature meat or seafood as ingredients, some use fish or oyster sauce or dried shrimp as flavourings. These can be adjusted for vegetarians by replacing the flavouring in question with a little more soy sauce or some yellow or black bean sauce. Freshness is all with vegetables: buy only the firmest, with the best colour and unblemished skins, and leaves that are shiny and with no signs of limpness. I cut vegetables like spring onions and courgettes at an angle to produce more interesting-looking pieces that cook faster. Never overcook vegetables, their crunchy textures are as important to the dish as their flavours.

Stir-fried Beansprouts

500 g / 1 lb beansprouts
2 garlic cloves
1 tablespoon oil
1 teaspoon sugar
1 tablespoon fish sauce

PREPARATION
Rinse the beansprouts lightly and pat dry.
Crush the garlic.

COOKING
Heat the oil in a wok or frying pan and stir-fry the garlic until aromatic.
Add the beansprouts and stir-fry quickly for a minute or two.
Stir in the sugar and fish sauce and serve.

Stir-fried Chinese Greens

500 g / 1 lb pak-choi *(see below)*
2 garlic cloves
1 tablespoon oil
1 tablespoon soy sauce, or more to taste

PREPARATION
Separate the pak-choi leaves, pile them on top of each other and slice in half lengthwise.
Slice the garlic thinly.

COOKING
Heat the oil in a wok or frying pan and stir-fry the garlic until aromatic.
Add the pak-choi and stir-fry over a highish heat until they become paler and slightly translucent.
Stir in the soy sauce and serve.

Pak-choi

Also known as Chinese mustard greens, pak-choi is a variety of Chinese cabbage. The thick white central ribs are wonderfully sweet and juicy and are good raw in salads, while the green leaves have a fine peppery flavour. It should never be boiled, but either steamed or stir-fried. Pak-choi is now widely available from better supermarkets. It has the great advantage of keeping well in the refrigerator.

Smoky Broccoli with Ginger

500 g / 1 lb broccoli
6 thin slices of ginger
1 tablespoon oil
1 tablespoon oyster sauce
4 tablespoons dry white wine

PREPARATION

Separate the broccoli stems from the florets. Peel the stems and cut them into slices. Separate the florets.
Slice the ginger into matchstick strips.

COOKING

Heat the oil in a wok or frying pan until very hot (almost smoking), then add the ginger and stir-fry briefly until aromatic.
Throw in the broccoli quickly and stir-fry briskly, adding in the oyster sauce, 2 tablespoons of water and the wine as you go.
Stir-fry for a further 5 minutes and serve.

Stir-fry Salad

2 medium carrots
200 g / 7 oz mange-tout peas
60 g / 2 oz beansprouts
1 garlic clove
2.5-cm / 1-inch piece of ginger, peeled
2 sprigs of basil
2 sprigs of coriander
2 tablespoons palm sugar *(see page 90)*
3 tablespoons black rice vinegar *(see below)*
3 tablespoons soy sauce
1 teaspoon five-spice powder *(see page 75)*
¼ teaspoon black pepper
1 tablespoon oil
1 tablespoon sesame seeds
2 tablespoons sesame oil

PREPARATION

Cut the carrots into bite-sized chunks.
Cut the mange-tout across in halves.
Rinse the beansprouts, if necessary, and pat dry.
Thinly slice the garlic and ginger.
Finely chop the basil and coriander.
Grate the palm sugar.
In a bowl, blend the sugar, garlic, ginger, vinegar, soy sauce, five-spice powder and pepper.

COOKING

Heat the oil in a wok or frying pan and stir-fry all the vegetables in sequence, stirring each well before adding the next.
Remove the vegetables from the wok or pan, transfer to a serving plate and pour the blended five-spice dressing over the top.
Dress with the sesame seeds and sesame oil.

Rice Vinegar

Characterized by its sweetness, Chinese rice vinegar comes in a wide variety of forms, pale, yellow or the rich dark black or Chinkiang rice vinegar – the balsamic vinegar of the East. If you can't find any, sweeten some white wine vinegar with a little sugar or maple syrup.

Stewed Tofu and Hard-boiled Eggs with Five-spice

200 g / 7 oz (¼ box) beancurd (*tofu, see page 110*)
6 small hard-boiled eggs
2 garlic cloves
1 red onion
2–3 spring onions
2–3 sprigs of coriander
2–3 tablespoons oil
1½ teaspoons five-spice powder (*see page 75*)
2 tablespoons soy sauce
2 tablespoons ketjap manis (*see page 92*)

PREPARATION

Drain the beancurd on a pile of paper towels, then cut into bite-sized chunks.
Shell the eggs and put them whole in a bowl.
Chop the garlic and red onion.
Chop the spring onions and coriander.

COOKING

Heat the oil in a wok or frying pan and shallow-fry the beancurd until lightly browned. Remove from the pan and put in a bowl.
In the same wok or pan, stir-fry the garlic, onion and five-spice powder until aromatic.
Add the beancurd back together with the eggs, soy sauce and ketjap manis. Stir well and add 1 small cup of water.
Bring to the boil, lower the heat and simmer for 20 minutes.
Serve garnished with spring onions and coriander.

Vegetarian Clay Pot

400 g / 14 oz (½ box) beancurd (*tofu, see page 110*)
115 g / 4 oz dried Chinese mushrooms
1 carrot
60 g / 2 oz bamboo shoots
1 red onion
1-cm / ½-inch piece of ginger, peeled
2 sprigs of coriander, for garnish
2 spring onions, for garnish
2 teaspoons cornflour
1 tablespoon oil
115 g / 4 oz baby sweetcorn
2 tablespoons soy sauce
2 tablespoons dry white wine
1 tablespoon sesame oil

PREPARATION

Slice the beancurd into 5-cm / 2-inch pieces. Leave to drain on a pile of paper towels.
Soak the Chinese mushrooms in boiling water for 5 minutes, then drain and chop.
Cut the carrot into bite-sized pieces.
Slice the bamboo shoots and onion.
Slice the ginger thinly.
Chop the coriander and spring onions.
In a small bowl, mix the cornflour with ½ small cup of water.

COOKING

Heat the oil in a clay pot (*see page 47*) and fry the beancurd lightly until browned. Remove and transfer to a plate.
In the same pot, fry the ginger and the Chinese mushrooms.
In stages, add all the vegetables in order, stirring in each before adding the next.
Stir well and add the soy sauce, dry white wine and cornflour mixture. Mix in well.
Return the beancurd to the pot, cover and simmer for about 10 minutes.
Remove from the heat, garnish with coriander and spring onions and dribble over the sesame oil.
Serve from the clay pot.

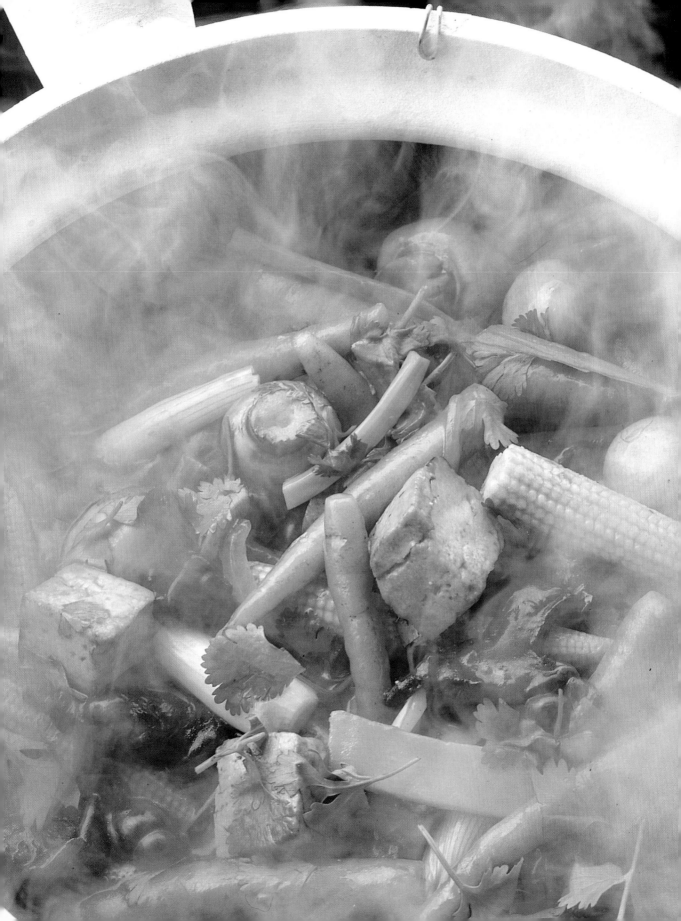

Tofu Curry

400 g / 14 oz (½ box) beancurd *(tofu, see below)*
1 large red onion
1 stalk of lemon grass *(see page 48)*
2–3 spring onions, for garnish
3–4 sprigs of coriander, for garnish
3 tablespoons oil
½ teaspoon ground cumin
1 teaspoon ground turmeric
1 tablespoon ground coriander
125 ml / 4 fl oz coconut milk
1 teaspoon salt

PREPARATION
Drain the beancurd on a pile of paper towels, then cut it into
12 pieces.
Grind the red onion coarsely.
Bash the lemon grass
Chop the spring onion and the coriander.

COOKING
Heat 1 tablespoon of oil in a wok or frying pan and stir-fry the
beancurd on all sides until lightly browned. Remove and set
aside on a plate.
Heat the remaining oil and stir-fry the onion and ground spices
over a moderate heat for 5 minutes.
Add in the lemon grass, beancurd, coconut milk, salt to taste and
½ a small cup of water and simmer for 10 minutes.
Serve hot, garnished with the spring onions and coriander.

Beancurd

Blocks of white fresh beancurd or tofu (its Japanese name),
extracted from yellow soya beans, are usually sold in plastic
trays in a little of their own liquid. These should be used
on the day of purchase, but can be kept for a few days if
the liquid is replaced with fresh water each day.
Beancurd usually needs to be cooked prior to eating
(sometimes it is sold ready-fried and golden), so it
first has to be well drained (normally on a pile of
paper towels) so that it will brown more readily. It is an
excellent source of vegetable protein and thus very
important to the vegetarian. Avoid Japanese
'silken tofu' for the recipes in this book, as it does
not hold up very well to being cooked.

Beancurd with Lemon and Lime Sauce

200 g / 7 oz (¼ box) beancurd *(tofu, see below)*
1 lemon
1 lime
1 garlic clove
1-cm / ½-inch piece of ginger, peeled
1 teaspoon cornflour
2 spring onions, for garnish
2–3 sprigs of coriander, for garnish
2 tablespoons oil
¼ teaspoon salt
1 tablespoon sugar
3 tablespoons ketjap manis *(see page 92)*

PREPARATION
Cut the beancurd into 4 pieces and leave to drain on a pile of
paper towels while you prepare everything else.
Squeeze the juice from the lemon and the lime.
Chop the garlic and the ginger.
Mix the cornflour to a paste with 1 small cup of water.
Chop the spring onions and coriander.

COOKING
In a wok, heat the oil over a moderate heat and fry the beancurd
until golden brown on all sides.
Add the garlic and ginger and stir well.
Then add the salt, sugar and the lemon and lime juices and stir
well.
Add the water and the cornflour and stir well. Leave to simmer
for 5 minutes.
Stir in the ketjap manis.
Transfer to serving plates and garnish with the
spring onions and coriander.

Stir-fried Rainbow Vegetables

100 g / 3½ oz carrots
100 g / 3½ oz courgettes
100 g / 3½ oz broccoli
100 g / 3½ oz colourful peppers
1 red onion
1 tablespoon oil
1 tablespoon oyster sauce
1 tablespoon soy sauce
1 tablespoon dry white wine

PREPARATION

Cut all the vegetables except the onion into bite-sized pieces.
Slice the onion.

COOKING

Heat the oil in a wok or frying pan and stir-fry the onion until lightly browned.
Add the vegetables in the order given above, stirring well before each next addition.
Stir well until thoroughly mixed, then add the oyster sauce and the soy sauce and a dash of water.
Cook for a further 1 minute, then add the wine.
Transfer to a plate to serve.

Pergedel Kentang
Potato Balls

3 large potatoes
115 g / 4 oz dried Chinese mushrooms
1 large onion
1 carrot
30 g / 1 oz bamboo shoots
2 tablespoons oil, plus more for shallow- or deep-frying balls
½ teaspoon salt
½ teaspoon black pepper
1 teaspoon sugar
2 teaspoons ground coriander
½ teaspoon ground turmeric
1 teaspoon garlic powder
2 teaspoons cornflour
1 egg, beaten
2 tablespoons plain flour
2 tablespoons sesame seeds

PREPARATION

Cook the potatoes in boiling salted water until tender. Drain well and mash, then chill in the refrigerator.
Soak the mushrooms in boiling water to cover for about 5 minutes, then drain and chop.
Chop the onion.
Dice the carrot.
Drain the bamboo shoots and dice them.

COOKING

Heat the oil in a wok or frying pan and stir-fry the onions until soft.
Add the mushrooms and carrot and stir-fry for 1 minute.
Add the bamboo shoots, salt, pepper, sugar, coriander, turmeric, garlic powder and cornflour. Stir-fry for a minute or two, then set aside off the heat.
Scoop up a tablespoonful of chilled mashed potato in the palm of the hand and flatten it.
Put a spoonful of the mushroom filling in the middle and roll the potato up around it, making a ball that totally encloses the filling.
Coat the balls with the egg and then the flour, before rolling them in sesame seeds and pressing them in well.
Shallow- or deep-fry the balls, in batches if necessary, until golden brown all over.
Serve hot or cold.

Tahu with Oyster Sauce

400 g / 14 oz (½ box) beancurd *(tofu, see page 110)*
2 garlic cloves
1 teaspoon cornflour
1 tablespoon oil
2 tablespoons oyster sauce

PREPARATION

Drain the beancurd on a pile of paper towels, then cut it into
1-cm / ½-inch cubes.
Crush the garlic.
In a small bowl, mix the cornflour with 2 tablespoons of water.

COOKING

Heat the oil in a wok or frying pan and stir-fry the garlic until
aromatic.
Add the beancurd and stir-fry for 1 minute.
Stir in the oyster sauce and cornflour mixture. Bring to a simmer
briefly.
Serve hot.

Sayur Satay, Kachang Sauce
Barbecued Vegetables with Peanut Sauce

3 small peppers *(1 red, 1 yellow and 1 green)*
1 large carrot
2½ cauliflower florets
1 chunky red onion
1 courgette
1 teaspoon garlic powder
¼ teaspoon ground turmeric
½ teaspoon salt
1 teaspoon sugar
2 tablespoons oil
palm or banana leaves to serve *(optional)*
12 satay sticks, about 10-15 cm / 4-6 inches long

FOR THE PEANUT SAUCE:

175 g / 6 oz dry-roasted peanuts
¼ teaspoon ground coriander
pinch of ground cumin
¼ teaspoon ground turmeric
½ teaspoon garlic powder
2 tablespoons sugar
1 teaspoon chilli oil *(optional)*

PREPARATION

Prepare all vegetables, trimming and deseeding as necessary.
Cut them into chunks.
In a large bowl, mix the garlic powder, turmeric, salt, sugar and
oil together. Add the vegetable chunks and toss to coat well in
the mixture. Just before you want to start cooking, thread them
on the satay sticks
With a pestle and mortar or in a food processor, blend the
peanuts for the sauce to a smooth paste.

COOKING

First make the sauce: in saucepan, mix the peanut paste with
1 small cup of water. Bring to the boil, lower the heat and add all
the remaining ingredients with salt to taste (be careful with the
salt as the peanuts are probably going to be quite salty
already!). Leave to simmer gently for 30 minutes. At the end of
cooking it should have a good thick pouring consistency; if it is
too thick, add a little more water.
When ready to eat, preheat a hot barbecue, grill or griddle and
cook the vegetables, in batches, until light brown. Do not let
them cook too long, to ensure that they still retain a little bite.
   Serve the cooked vegetables on palm or banana leaves, if
you like, with the warm peanut sauce.

Goreng Sayur
Deep-fried Vegetables

-

2 cauliflower florets
2 broccoli florets
1 medium carrot
1 medium onion
150 g / 5 oz self-raising flour
1 teaspoon salt
oil for deep-frying
12 satay sticks, about 10–15 cm / 4–6 inches long

PREPARATION
Cut the vegetables into chunky bite-sized pieces.
Skewer alternating vegetable chunks on the satay sticks.
Sift the flour and salt into a large bowl. Add 125 ml / 4 fl oz water and whisk it in slowly, then beat it more vigorously to make a smooth batter.

COOKING
Heat the oil for deep-frying. Dip the skewered vegetables in the batter and deep-fry in batches until golden brown.
Serve hot.

Sambal Egg

6 hard-boiled eggs
2 red onions
4 red chillies
1 teaspoon tamarind pulp *(see page 38)*
2 tablespoons oil
1 tablespoon sugar
½ teaspoon salt

PREPARATION
Shell the eggs and cut them into halves.
In a food processor, grind 1 of the onions and all the chillies. Slice the other onion.
Soak the tamarind pulp in 3 tablespoons of hot water and squeeze to extract the juice. Discard pulp and reserve the juice.

COOKING
Heat the oil in a stainless-steel or non-stick wok or frying pan and stir-fry the onion and chillies for 5 minutes over a moderate heat.
Add the tamarind juice, sugar and salt. Fry for 2 minutes more.
Arrange the egg halves and onion slices on plates and pour the hot sambal mixture over.

Chillies

Green chillies and their riper red counterparts are used both as an ingredient in cooking and as a garnish. As well as imparting their own richly aromatic flavour and their heat, they also seem to have the power to bring out the flavours of other ingredients around them in a dish. For this sort of cooking try to seek out the short thin Thai or 'bird' peppers. Look for peppers that are crisp and firm, with no wrinkles or blemishes. Those of us who are used to chilli heat tend to use the entire pepper, even when they are chopped or sliced. However, those not used to chillies are probably best advised to remove the seeds and the pale membrane to which they are attached inside the peppers, as these are the hottest parts. Take great care when handling peppers not to touch the face, etc., and wash you hands well immediately afterwards.

Okra Salad

Vegetarians can replace the dried shrimp with the same weight of dried Chinese mushrooms or cashew nuts. Deal with the mushrooms in exactly the same way as you would the dried shrimp, but the cashew nuts should simply be briefly dry-fried and sprinkled over the dish at the end.

500 g / 1 lb okra *(see opposite)*
2 lemons
115 g / 4 oz dried shrimp
2 red chillies
1 teaspoon salt
1 tablespoon sugar

PREPARATION

Top and tail the okra.
Squeeze the juice from the lemons.
Wash the dried shrimp and soak in ½ a small cup of boiling water for 5 minutes to soften and then drain, reserving the water.
Roughly pound the chillies and the shrimp. Put in a mixing bowl.
Add the lemon juice, the reserved shrimp-soaking water, salt and sugar. Mix well.

COOKING

Steam the okra for 10 minutes in a bamboo steamer, then remove and transfer to a serving plate.
Pour the prawn mixture on top and serve.

Savoury Pineapple and Coriander Salad

1 whole pineapple
10 sprigs of coriander
1 chilli
2 shallots
2 small garlic cloves
1 lime
2–3 tablespoons fish sauce
1 teaspoon sugar
2 tablespoons sesame oil
1 tablespoon sesame seeds, for garnish
handful of cashew nuts, for garnish

PREPARATION

Cut the pineapple lengthwise into 4 quarter segments and remove the core.
Using a flexible knife, cut the flesh away from the skins to leave 4 shells. Cut the flesh into cubes, then place in a bowl.
Finely chop most of the coriander, reserving a few whole leaves for garnish.
Pound the chilli, shallots and garlic.
Squeeze the juice from the lime.
Add the chopped coriander, fish sauce, sugar and sesame oil to the pineapple flesh in the bowl and mix well.
Add the chilli, the shallots, the garlic and the lime juice and stir again.
Pile the mixture back in the hollowed-out pineapple shells.
Garnish with sesame seeds, reserved coriander leaves and cashew nuts.

Cucumber Pickle with Onion Rings

1 cucumber
2 teaspoons salt
1 red chilli
1 onion
2 tablespoons white malt vinegar
1½ tablespoons sugar

PREPARATION

Cut the cucumber into thin rounds. Add 1 teaspoon of salt to the cucumber, mix well and let stand for 10 minutes in a colander to drain the excess water.
Slice the chilli thinly.
Slice the onion and separate into rings.

COOKING

In a large serving bowl, mix the cucumber, chilli and onion. Mix well.
In a small bowl, mix the vinegar, sugar and the remaining salt with ½ a small cup of water. Pour this over the cucumber to serve.

Okra

Also know as ladies' fingers, these have a wonderful flavour and are filled with edible seeds in sticky juices that act as a natural thickening agent for any dish in which they are used. Look for smallish firm glossy pods with no hints of brown at the tips. If using them whole, be careful when removing the stalk end not to break into the interior of the pod or you will lose the juices. Okra is highly nutritious, rich in vegetable protein and folic acid, and the juices are said to soothe the gut.

Baked Aubergine in Yellow Bean Sauce

1 large aubergine
1 large onion
2 garlic cloves
2 red chillies
2 tomatoes
2 sprigs of coriander
1 spring onion
2 tablespoons oil
2 tablespoons yellow bean sauce

PREPARATION

Cut the aubergine in half lengthwise. Scoop out the inner flesh, leaving a shell with a thickness of about 1 cm / ½ inch, and reserve the flesh. Soak the shells in cold water for about 20 minutes to get rid of any bitterness and prevent discoloration. Chop the onion, garlic, chillies, tomatoes and coriander. Thinly slice the spring onion.

COOKING

Heat the oil in a wok or frying pan and stir-fry the onion and garlic for about 2 minutes.
Add the yellow bean sauce and aubergine flesh and stir-fry for 2 minutes.
Add the tomatoes, chillies, coriander and spring onion. Stir-fry for 5 minutes more.
Transfer the contents of the wok or pan to a plate and leave to cool.
Preheat the oven to 190°C/375°F/gas 5.
Drain the aubergine shells and pat dry. Fill them with the cooled mixture and bake in the oven for about 15-20 minutes (if at any time the top seems to be browning too fast, cover it loosely with a piece of foil).

Yellow Bean Sauce

Yellow bean sauce or paste is very much like black bean sauce, but made from yellow beans. It is often used in chicken and pork dishes and goes well with ginger.

Deep-fried Aubergine

1 large aubergine
150 g / 5 oz self-raising flour
pinch of salt
½ teaspoon pepper
1 teaspoon garlic powder
oil for deep-frying

PREPARATION

Cut the aubergine across into slices about 1 cm / ½ inch thick. If you like, you can then make this dish more decorative by using pastry cutters – try star shapes, sun shapes or moon shapes or anything that takes your fancy.
Soak the slices in cold water briefly to remove any bitterness and prevent discoloration.
Sift the flour into a large mixing bowl. Add the salt, pepper and garlic powder, followed by 125 ml / 4 fl oz water. Whisk vigorously until you have a smooth batter and leave for 15 minutes to rest.
Drain the aubergine slices and pat dry with paper towels.

COOKING

Heat the oil for deep-frying. Dip the slices of aubergine in the batter and deep-fry in batches until golden brown. Drain on paper towels.
Serve while still hot and crisp.

Aubergines

The aubergine, a relative of the potato and tomato, has a fine meaty texture and an ability to absorb and blend strong flavours. In the West, the big purple rugby balls are the norm. In the east, however, different varieties are to be found, from the long thin Japanese type to the little round ones that may be white in colour (hence the American name for the aubergine, 'eggplant'). Look for fine well-rounded aubergines with taut unwrinkled and unblemished skins. Leave the skins on as they are quite digestible and highly nutritious.

Canoodling...

Rice and Noodles

Rice and noodles are our staples in Southeast Asia – our bread and potatoes – supplying the all-important starch that the body needs as fuel. One of the reasons for our prolific use of flavourings, particularly chillies, is to help us consume large quantities of these fuel foods. Many of the dishes in this chapter make excellent one-pot meals for one or two people, as well as serving as good fillers in a more complex meal for larger numbers. Be careful when storing cooked rice for use in the rice dishes: it needs to be kept in the refrigerator or it can fall prey to potentially troublesome bacteria. Uncooked rice, however, will keep for years without any significant deterioration.

Coriander and Spring Onion Fried Rice

2 spring onions
2 sprigs of coriander
1 tablespoon oil
500 g / 1 lb cooked rice
1½ tablespoons soy sauce

PREPARATION
Slice the spring onions.
Chop the coriander finely.

COOKING
Heat the oil in a wok or frying pan, then add the rice and soy sauce.
Stir-fry well until piping hot.
Add the spring onions and the coriander.
Stir for a further minute and transfer to a serving plate.
Serve hot.

Rainbow Rice

¼ each red, orange and green peppers
1 red chilli
1 small carrot
2 spring onions
½ small red onion
100 g / 3½ oz lean steak
100 g / 3½ oz peeled cooked prawns
2 tablespoons oil
1 egg, beaten
500 g / 1 lb cooked rice
1 tablespoon oyster sauce
1 tablespoon soy sauce

PREPARATION
Deseed the peppers and chop them finely.
Finely chop the chilli, carrot, spring onions and red onion.
Slice the steak thinly across the grain and chop the prawns finely.

COOKING
Heat the oil in a wok or frying pan and stir-fry all the chopped vegetables over a high heat.
Add the prawns and steak and stir-fry for 5 minutes.
Add the egg and stir-fry quickly to scramble it.
Add the rice and continue to stir-fry until the rice is piping hot.
Finally add the oyster sauce and soy sauce and toss well until evenly mixed.
Serve immediately.

Cooking Rice

I always use long-grain rice or Thai fragrant rice (which, though more expensive, has a lovely flavour). For every 2 cups of rice (to serve 4 people), measure out 2½-3 cups of cold water (the Thai rice needs slightly less water) into a pan, add the rice and bring to the boil. Then lower the heat to a gentle simmer, cover tightly and cook for 15 minutes until all the water has been absorbed and the rice is tender.

Fried Rice with Nuts

60 g / 2 oz cashew nuts
30 g / 1 oz almonds
30 g / 1 oz peanuts *(optional)*
1 spring onion
1 chilli *(optional)*
1½ tablespoons oil
1 egg
500 g / 1 lb cooked rice
2 tablespoons soy sauce
¼ teaspoon pepper

PREPARATION
Toast the nuts in a dry frying pan over a moderate heat, shaking
frequently, until lightly browned.
Chop the spring onion and the chilli for garnish, if using.

COOKING
Heat the oil in a wok or frying pan and add the egg. Stir-fry
quickly until lightly scrambled.
Add the rice, soy sauce and pepper and stir-fry until piping hot.
Place the rice on a serving plate and sprinkle with the toasted
nuts, spring onion and chilli, if using.

Nasi Ayam
Chicken and Chilli Fried Rice

300 g / 10½ oz skinless chicken breast fillet
1 chilli
1 garlic clove
2 tablespoons oil
500 g / 1 lb cooked rice
1 egg
1 tablespoon oyster sauce
1 tablespoon soy sauce

PREPARATION
Slice the chicken into small cubes.
Chop the chilli and garlic.

COOKING
Heat the oil in a wok or frying pan and stir-fry the chicken for
about 5 minutes until cooked through.
Add the rice and egg and stir well quickly until the egg is
scrambled.
Add the chilli and garlic and both the sauces. Stir well and serve.

Beef Fried Rice

300 g / 10½ oz fillet steak
2 teaspoons cornflour
1 teaspoon fish sauce
1 teaspoon oyster sauce
1 teaspoon garlic powder
½ teaspoon pepper
2 thin slices of ginger
4 spring onions
2–3 sprigs of coriander, for garnish
2 tablespoons oil
500 g / 1 lb cooked rice

PREPARATION
Slice the steak thinly across the grain and then chop the slices into matchstick shreds.
In a large bowl, mix the cornflour, fish sauce, oyster sauce, garlic powder and pepper. Toss the steak in this mixture to season it and leave to marinate for 30 minutes.
Slice the ginger.
Chop the spring onions and coriander.

COOKING
Heat the oil in a wok or frying pan and stir-fry the sliced ginger until aromatic.
Add the marinated steak and stir-fry until lightly browned.
Add the rice and stir-fry until piping hot.
Transfer to a serving plate and garnish with the spring onions and coriander.

Onion Rice

2 spring onions
1 small red onion
1 small white onion
4 shallots
2 red chillies
2 sprigs of coriander, for garnish
thin wedge of cucumber, for garnish
2 tablespoons oil
1 teaspoon garlic powder
500 g / 1 lb cooked rice
2 tablespoons fish sauce
1 tablespoon oyster sauce
½ teaspoon black pepper

PREPARATION
Slice the spring onions, both onions, shallots and chillies.
Chop the coriander and slice the cucumber.

COOKING
Heat the oil in a wok or frying pan and stir-fry the spring onions, onions and shallots until golden brown.
Add the garlic powder, chillies and rice and stir-fry for a good 5 minutes.
Stir in the fish sauce, oyster sauce and black pepper.
Garnish with cucumber and coriander to serve.

Egg Fried Rice

4 spring onions
1 teaspoon oil
1 egg, beaten
500 g / 1 lb cooked rice
2 tablespoons soy sauce

PREPARATION
Chop the spring onions.

COOKING
Heat the oil in a wok or frying pan and stir-fry the spring onions until lightly browned.
Add the egg and stir-fry quickly until scrambled.
Add the rice and soy sauce and stir-fry until piping hot.
Transfer to a serving plate.

Nasi Udang
Prawn Fried Rice

115 g / 4 oz prawns
1 garlic clove
1 chilli
1 tablespoon oil
1 egg, beaten
500 g / 1 lb cooked rice
1 tablespoon soy sauce

PREPARATION
Peel and devein the prawns *(see page 33)*. Chop them into chunks.
Chop the garlic and pound the chilli to a paste.

COOKING
Heat the oil in a wok or frying pan and stir-fry the garlic with the prawns and the egg quickly until scrambled.
Add the rice, soy sauce and chilli paste and stir-fry until piping hot.
Serve immediately.

Nasi Lemak
Coconut Rice

500 g / 1 lb rice
¼ teaspoon salt
1 pandan leaf *(see below)*
125 ml / 4 fl oz coconut milk

COOKING
In a large pan, bring 2 small cups of water to the boil with the salt and pandan leaf.
When it is boiling, add the rice and stir once.
Then add the coconut milk, stir again and bring back to the boil.
Cover the pan tightly, lower the heat to a very gentle simmer and cook for 10 minutes undisturbed.

Pandan Leaves

Pandan or pandanus leaves are the leaves of the screw pine (actually a type of palm tree) and are used to add a green colour and a lovely grassy flowery flavour to food (more usually sweet). Pandan leaves are increasingly available from Oriental food markets. Look for leaves with one side still shiny, as this dulls with age.

Mee Sayur
Vegetable Noodles with Oyster Sauce

2 small nests of dried egg noodles
½ carrot
½ courgette
4 French beans
2 cauliflower florets
2 broccoli florets
1 tablespoon oil
1 tablespoon oyster sauce
2 tablespoons fish sauce
1 small cup of stock or water

PREPARATION

Soak the noodles in boiling water for 1 minute. Drain in a colander and rinse well under cold running water. Squeeze out any excess water.
Slice the carrot across into thin rounds.
Halve the courgette and slice.
Chop the beans.
Cut the cauliflower and broccoli into bite-sized pieces.

COOKING

Heat the oil a wok or frying pan and stir-fry the noodles until piping hot.
Add all the vegetables and stir-fry for 2 minutes.
Stir in the oyster and fish sauces, then pour in the stock or water around the edge of the pan.
Toss well briefly over a high heat and serve.

The Various Types of Noodle

Of the many types of noodles used throughout Southeast Asia, I only really use the following:

Rice vermicelli – small wiry-looking noodles made from rice flour, which are usually sold dried. They are very easily broken and need careful long soaking in cold water (hot water makes them too soggy) and careful draining.

Medium flat rice flour noodles – looking rather like thin tagliatelle.

Dried egg noodles – yellow noodles, looking like spaghetti, usually sold curled into 'nests', which should be encouraged apart during soaking and/or cooking. After soaking or pre-cooking they need to be well drained – even squeezed to remove excess moisture – before frying.

Fresh noodles – treat like fresh pasta.

Oil noodles – ready cooked, so these need no preparation.

Mee Daging
Beef Egg Noodles

Dealing with noodles in a pan is one occasion when chopsticks really come in handy in the kitchen. You'll find they are much more effective for moving noodles about in a pan than any scoop, ladle or spoon.

175 g / 6 oz lean beef fillet
1 tablespoon oyster sauce
1 tablespoon soy sauce
½ teaspoon pepper
1 teaspoon cornflour
150 g / 5 oz rice vermicelli
2 garlic cloves
1½ tablespoons oil
150 ml / ¼ pint stock

PREPARATION

Slice the beef thinly across the grain.
In a large bowl, mix the oyster sauce, soy sauce, pepper and cornflour. Toss the beef in this mixture to season it.
Soak the vermicelli in cold water until just soft, then drain well.
Chop the garlic.

COOKING

Heat half the oil in a wok or frying pan and stir-fry the noodles for 5 minutes until lightly browned. Transfer to a plate.
Heat the remaining oil and stir-fry the garlic and seasoned beef for 1 minute.
Add the stock and stir.
Return the noodles to the wok or pan and toss until piping hot.

Bakmie Goreng
Fried Egg Noodles with Mixed Meats

2 nests of dried egg noodles
85 g / 3 oz prawns
85 g / 3 oz lean pork
85 g / 3 oz skinless boned chicken meat
2 garlic cloves
2 spring onions
2-3 sprigs of coriander
500 g / 1 lb Chinese cabbage
2 tablespoons oil
2 eggs, beaten
½ small cup of stock or water
4 tablespoons ketjap manis *(see page 92)*
115 g / 4 oz beansprouts *(optional)*

FOR THE DIP:
5 chillies
3-4 tablespoons soy sauce

PREPARATION
Soak the noodles in boiling water for 1 minute.
Drain in a colander and rinse well. Squeeze out any excess water.
Peel and devein the prawns *(see page 33)*. Cut them in halves.
Slice the pork and chicken.
Crush the garlic and chop the spring onions and coriander.
Shred the cabbage.
Chop the chillies for the dip and mix them with the soy sauce.

COOKING
Heat the oil in a wok or frying pan and stir-fry the garlic, prawns, pork and chicken for about 5 minutes until cooked through.
Add the eggs and continue to stir-fry quickly over a high heat until they are scrambled.
Add the noodles and stir well.
Pour in the stock around the sides of the pan and toss the noodles again.
Stir in half the ketjap manis, followed by the cabbage. Stir well and add the beansprouts, if using.
Transfer to a serving plate and dribble over the remaining ketjap manis. Garnish with the coriander and spring onions and serve with the chilli dip.

Pickled Fish Noodles

100 g / 3½ oz rice vermicelli *(see introduction to Chap Chye, opposite)*
1 chilli
30 g / 1 oz pickled fish
1 teaspoon sugar
1 garlic clove
2 spring onions
2 sprigs of coriander
1½ tablespoons oil
2 thin slices of ginger
½ small cup of stock or water
2 tablespoons oyster sauce
½ teaspoon pepper, or to taste
1 teaspoon sugar, or to taste
150 g / 5 oz beansprouts
½ lemon
1 tablespoon soy sauce

PREPARATION
Soak the vermicelli in cold water for 30 minutes and then drain.
Finely chop the chilli.
Separate the flakes of fish and remove any bones. Sprinkle it with the sugar and chopped chilli. Leave to marinate while you prepare the rest of the ingredients.
Chop the garlic, spring onions and coriander.

COOKING
Heat 1 tablespoon of oil in a wok or frying pan and stir-fry the vermicelli for 2 minutes. Transfer to a plate and set aside.
Heat the remaining oil in the wok or frying pan and stir-fry the garlic and ginger until aromatic.
Add the fish and stir-fry briefly.
Add the stock or water around the edge of the pan and bring to the boil. Return the vermicelli to the pan and toss well.
Stir in the oyster sauce, pepper and sugar to taste.
Add the beansprouts and stir-fry for about 30 seconds.
Transfer to a serving plate, squeeze over the juice from the lemon and sprinkle over the soy sauce. Garnish with the spring onions and coriander to serve.

Chap Chye

When using rice vermicelli, you have to learn exactly how long to soak them by trial and error as some types get soft more quickly than others. Never use hot water to soak them as they then get far too soft and become unworkable.

150 g / 5 oz rice vermicelli
60 g / 2 oz mixed dried mushrooms
30 g / 1 oz beancurd *(tofu, see page 110)*
1 carrot
225 g / 8 oz cabbage
30 g / 1 oz fresh mushrooms
30 g / 1 oz French beans
2 sprigs of coriander
2 tablespoons oil
1 teaspoon sugar
3 tablespoons soy sauce
1 teaspoon pepper
1 tablespoon chilli sauce

PREPARATION
Soak the vermicelli in cold water until soft. Drain well.
Soak the dried mushrooms in boiling water for 5 minutes. Drain and thinly slice.
Put the beancurd to drain on a pile of paper towels. Cut into cubes.
Slice the carrot into matchstick shreds.
Thinly slice the cabbage, fresh mushrooms and beans.
Chop the coriander for garnish.

COOKING
Heat half the oil in a wok or frying pan and fry the beancurd until lightly browned all over. Remove and set aside.
Heat the remaining oil and stir-fry the cabbage, carrots and beans for 2 minutes.
Add both types of mushroom and stir-fry for 2 minutes.
Add the sugar, soy sauce, pepper and ½ a small cup of water and stir-fry over a high heat for 2 more minutes.
Add the vermicelli and stir-fry until piping hot.
Serve sprinkled with a little chilli sauce and sprinkled with the coriander and beancurd.

Pad Met Krob
Rice Vermicelli with Prawns

150 g / 5 oz rice vermicelli
175 g / 6 oz prawns
2 garlic cloves
115 g / 4 oz cabbage
2 sprigs of coriander, for garnish
2 tablespoons oil
1 tablespoon fish sauce
1 tablespoon soy sauce
½ teaspoon pepper
1 small cup of stock or water
150 g / 5 oz beansprouts *(optional)*

PREPARATION
Soak the vermicelli in cold water until just soft *(see left)*. Drain well.
Peel and devein the prawns *(see page 33)*.
Crush the garlic and slice the cabbage into shreds.
Chop the coriander.

COOKING
Heat half the oil in a wok or frying pan and stir-fry the vermicelli for 5 minutes. Remove from the pan and set aside.
Heat the remaining oil and stir-fry the garlic until aromatic.
Add the cabbage, prawns, fish sauce, soy sauce and pepper, and stir-fry for 5 minutes.
Add the stock or water round the edge of the pan and return the vermicelli to the pan. Stir-fry briefly.
Stir in the beansprouts over a high heat, if using, toss well and serve garnished with the coriander.

Mee Goreng
Fried Noodles Indian-style

150 g / 5 oz oil noodles or spaghetti
2 tablespoon oil, plus more for the spaghetti if using
115 g / 4 oz prawns or skinless boned chicken meat
115 g / 4 oz cabbage
1 small tomato
1 small onion
10-cm / 4-inch piece of celery
2–3 sprigs of coriander, for garnish
2 garlic cloves
1 chilli
½ boiled potato
2 tablespoons oil
1 egg, beaten
1 tablespoon tomato ketchup
2 tablespoons soy sauce
¼ teaspoon salt
½ teaspoon sugar
115 g / 4 oz beansprouts
1 lemon

PREPARATION
If using spaghetti, cook it in boiling salted water until just tender, then drain well and toss in a tablespoon of oil to keep it from sticking together. There is no need to prepare the oil noodles.
Peel and devein the prawns *(see page 33)*, if using them, and chop. Dice the chicken if using that.
Slice the cabbage and tomato.
Chop the onion, celery and coriander.
Crush the garlic and the chilli.
Dice the cooked potato.

COOKING
Heat the oil in a wok or frying pan and fry the garlic, onion, cabbage, celery, potato and prawns or chicken.
Add the noodles and stir-fry for 10 minutes more.
Make a gap in the centre of the noodles and add the egg and stir it in to scramble it.
Add the chilli, tomato, tomato ketchup, soy sauce, salt and sugar. Stir well.
Just before transferring it to a serving plate, add the beansprouts and stir for about 30 seconds.
Sprinkle over the juice from the lemon and the chopped coriander to serve.

Hokkien Mee
Oil Noodles with Seafood & Pork Malaysian-style

60 g / 2 oz prawns
60 g / 2 oz skinless boned chicken
60 g / 2 oz pork fillet
3 garlic cloves
1 chilli
2 tablespoons oil
500 g / 1 lb oil noodles
1 teaspoon salt
2 tablespoons soy sauce
1 large ladleful of stock or water
115 g / 4 oz beansprouts
lemon wedges, to serve

PREPARATION
Peel and devein the prawns *(see page 33)*. Chop them in half.
Slice the chicken and pork across the grain into thin strips.
Chop the garlic and slice the chilli.

COOKING
Heat the oil in a wok or frying pan and stir-fry the garlic until aromatic.
Then, in the order given, add the pork, chicken and prawns in sequence, stir-frying each for 1 minute before adding the next.
Add the noodles with the salt and soy sauce and stir-fry until piping hot. Pour in the stock or water around the edge of the pan.
Just before serving, stir in the beansprouts.
Turn out on a serving plate, garnish with the sliced chilli and serve with lemon wedges.

Crispy Noodles

150 g / 5 oz rice vermicelli
275 g / 10 oz firm fish fillets (like monkfish or halibut)
2 tablespoons fish sauce
¼ teaspoon sugar
1 teaspoon cornflour
oil for deep-frying

PREPARATION

Soak the vermicelli in cold water to make them pliable and drain them well.
Cut the fish into cubes.

COOKING

Deep-fry the vermicelli until crisp, transfer to a serving plate and keep warm.
Heat 1 tablespoon of the oil in a wok or frying pan and stir-fry the fish for 5 minutes.
Add a ladleful of water and, keeping the heat high, add the fish sauce, sugar and cornflour. Stir-fry until the liquid thickens.
Pour the contents of the pan over the vermicelli and serve.

Egg Noodles with Chicken and Vegetables

2 nests of dried egg noodles
225 g / 8 oz skinless chicken breast fillet
4 broccoli florets
½ courgette
¼ red pepper
5-cm / 2-inch piece of ginger, peeled
2 tablespoons oil
2 tablespoons soy sauce
2 tablespoons oyster sauce
½ teaspoon black pepper
2 teaspoons cornflour
handful of crushed peanuts

PREPARATION

Soak the noodles in boiling water for 1 minute. Drain in a colander and rinse with cold water. Squeeze out excess water.
Slice the chicken across the grain into thin pieces.
Slice the broccoli, courgette and red pepper.
Chop the ginger.

COOKING

Heat the oil in a wok or frying pan and stir-fry the ginger until aromatic.
Add the chicken and stir-fry for 5 minutes until cooked.
Add the sliced vegetables and stir well, while pouring in a ladleful of water around the edge.
Make a well in the middle of the pan and add the noodles. Stir-fry for 5 minutes.
Add the soy sauce, oyster sauce, black pepper and the cornflour. Stir well for a further 2 minutes.
Serve garnished with the crushed peanuts.

Bhud Thai

Flat Noodles with Prawns and Chicken

150 g / 5 oz dried flat rice noodles
115 g / 4 oz pork fillet
115 g / 4 oz prawns
2 tablespoons tamarind pulp
2 garlic cloves
1 chilli
2.5-cm / 1-inch length of lemon grass *(see page 48)*
2 spring onions
60 g / 2 oz peanuts
2 tablespoons oil
1 egg
3 tablespoons fish sauce
½ small cup of stock or water
1 tablespoon sugar
60 g / 2 oz beansprouts

PREPARATION

Being careful not to break them, soak the noodles in cold water
(they take a long time to soften!). Drain well when they are fully
softened.
Slice the pork across the grain into very thin slices.
Peel and devein the prawns *(see page 33)*.
Soak the tamarind pulp in ½ a small cup of water. Squeeze and
drain. Then discard the tamarind pulp.
Crush the garlic and the chilli.
Bash the lemon grass.
Slice the spring onions into 2.5-cm / 1-inch pieces.
Grind the peanuts to a coarse powder.

COOKING

Heat the oil in a stainless steel or non-stick wok or frying pan
and stir-fry the garlic until aromatic.
Add the lemon grass, garlic, pork, prawns, chilli and the egg, and
stir-fry well for about 5 minutes.
Add the noodles and continue to stir.
Add the fish sauce, tamarind juice, stock or water, sugar and half
the spring onions and stir well.
Lastly stir in the beansprouts and transfer to a serving plate.
Serve garnished with the ground peanuts and remaining spring
onions.

Noodles with Mushrooms

150 g / 5 oz rice vermicelli
115 g / 4 oz mixed dried mushrooms
30 g / 1 oz fresh mushrooms
1 carrot
115 g / 4 oz cabbage
30 g / 1 oz French beans
2 sprigs of coriander
30 g / 1 oz beancurd *(tofu, see page 110)*
1 tablespoon oil
1 tablespoon soy sauce
1 teaspoon sugar
1 teaspoon pepper
2 tablespoons chilli sauce

PREPARATION

Soak the vermicelli in cold water for 30 minutes. Drain well.
Soak the dried mushrooms in hot water for 5 minutes. Drain well
and chop.
Slice all the vegetables and chop the coriander.
Drain the beancurd on a pile of paper towels. Chop it into bite-
sized cubes.

COOKING

Heat the oil in a wok or frying pan and stir-fry the beancurd until
lightly browned. Remove and set aside.
Add in the dried and fresh mushrooms with the rest of the
vegetables and stir-fry for about 3 minutes.
Add in 1 small cup of water and the vermicelli. Stir well over a
high heat.
Stir in the beancurd, soy sauce, sugar and pepper.
Serve dressed with a little chilli sauce and garnished with the
coriander.

Rice girls do it under water!

7 Desserts

Desserts are not a big deal in Southeast Asia, rich spicy meals usually ending with fresh fruit. Of course there is a great tradition of sweet snacks and street food, usually little cakes and pancakes, etc. Even in sweet dishes, rice plays a big part, especially glutinous rice, varieties of rice that have a lovely chewy sticky quality when cooked and so readily form into balls, cakes or fritters without any binding medium. Sweet rice cakes are usually steamed or fried. A lot of our sweet dishes are also traditional at breakfast and some of those that follow you might like to try instead of unhealthy bacon and eggs – Ben's favourite!

Bobo Pulot Hitam
Black Glutinous Rice

300 g / 10½ oz black glutinous rice *(see below)*
150 g / 5 oz sugar
2 pinches of salt
225 ml / 8 fl oz coconut milk

PREPARATION
Measure the rice in a measuring jug. Tip it into a bowl and set aside.

COOKING
Measure into a large pan 4 times the volume of water as there is rice. Bring to the boil and add the rice.
When it returns to the boil, turn the heat down low and simmer for 1 hour.
Add sugar and salt to taste (if you add these earlier the rice doesn't cook as well).
Just before serving, stir in the coconut milk.

Black Glutinous Rice

Also known as Japonica or Thai black rice, this variety of glutinous or sticky rice is actually a very deep purple in colour. Apart from its colour (which seeps dramatically into the cooking water) and its lovely grassy flavour, it is unusual for a glutinous rice in being long-grain. It has recently become very trendy in the USA and is now quite widely available in Oriental supermarkets.

Star Fruit with Lime Sauce

2 star fruit *(see below)*
1 lime
2 pieces of rock sugar *(see page 140)*

PREPARATION
Slice the star fruit and put the slices in a serving bowl.
Squeeze the juice from the lime.

COOKING
In a small heavy-based pan, melt the rock sugar over a low heat.
Stir in the lime juice.
Pour over the star fruit and serve.

Star Fruit

The lantern-shaped star fruit, carambola or belimbing is a type of tree melon that is grown all over Asia. When sliced it produces very attractive star-shaped slices that can decorate any sweet dish. There are two types: the smaller is fairly tart and lemony in flavour, while the larger – with thick juicy yellowish ribs – is sweeter and can have a lovely indefinable flavour like the best of melons. Buy firm fruit 7.5-12.5 cm / 3-5 inches in length, with no trace of brown on them.

Banana in Coconut Sauce

3 ripe bananas
225 ml / 8 fl oz coconut milk
2 tablespoons sugar
pinch of salt

PREPARATION
Peel and slice the bananas.

COOKING
In a saucepan, mix the coconut milk with the sugar and salt.
Add the sliced bananas and simmer for 5 minutes.
Serve hot.

Rock Sugar

Also known as lump or yellow sugar, this is a crystalline form of concentrated sugar that is sold as little rocks or blocks. Its rich caramel flavour is very popular in Chinese desserts and drinks, and rock sugar can be found in most Oriental supermarkets. Use dark brown sugar or maple syrup if you can't get a hold of any.

Pancakes Stuffed with Coconut

115 g / 4 oz plain flour
2 eggs
pinch of salt
½ teaspoon sugar
300 ml / ½ pint milk
drop of green colouring
1 tablespoon oil
ice-cream, to serve *(optional)*

FOR THE FILLING:
1 small cup of desiccated coconut
pinch of salt
2 tablespoon brown sugar

PREPARATION
Sieve the flour into a large bowl.
Add the eggs, salt, sugar, milk and a drop of green colouring.
Whisk to a smooth batter, mix in the oil and leave to stand for half an hour.

COOKING
First make the filling: bring 350 ml / 12 fl oz of water to the boil in a pan and add the coconut, salt and sugar. Simmer over a moderate heat for 20 minutes.
Heat a dry pancake pan until quite hot and add 2 tablespoons of the batter. Tilt the pan all round so that the batter spreads to cover the bottom of the pan.
Cook until bubbles rise on the top of the pancake, then turn it over (it should be nicely browned on the underside) and cook the other side until it is also lightly browned. Remove the pancake from the pan and transfer to a plate.
Wipe the pan clean with a wad of paper towels and continue cooking pancakes in the same way until the batter is all used up.
Fill each pancake with a teaspoon of filling, fold over and serve hot with or without ice-cream.

Sweet Potato with Ginger

500 g / 1 lb sweet potatoes *(see below)*
5-cm / 2-inch piece of ginger, peeled
2 tablespoons rock sugar *(see page 140)*

Preparation
Peel the sweet potatoes and cut them into bite-sized chunks.
Crush the ginger.

Cooking
Bring a pan of water to the boil and boil the sweet potatoes and ginger for 5 minutes.
Add the rock sugar and continue to boil until the sweet potatoes are soft, 10-15 minutes more.
Serve with the cooking liquid.

Sweet Potatoes

Although originally from Central America, these are now grown all over the tropics. There are several varieties with yellowish, pinkish, red or purple skins, but they fall into two main types: one with drier mealier yellowish flesh and the other with softer more moist white flesh. The latter are sweeter and are more popular in the East. They are cooked like potatoes, mostly boiled or baked in their skins. Choose plump sweet potatoes with unwrinkled skins.

Mixed Fruit Delight

1 whole pineapple
1 ripe papaya
1 honey melon
1-2 star fruit
1-2 mango(es)
1-2 orange(s)
1-2 guava(s)
1-2 passion fruit
1 lemon

Preparation
Wash and skin or top and tail the fruits, removing any seeds or stones as necessary. Cut them into bite-sized pieces.
Squeeze the juice from the lemon.
Arrange the fruits on a large platter and sprinkle the lemon juice over them.
Serve.

Cutting up Mangoes

Buy heavy firm mangoes that just yield to pressure and have a fine perfumed scent, with no hint of fermentation in it. To get the flesh most easily from a ripe mango, cut down through the fruit lengthwise on either side of the stone. Take the two round sections you have removed and cut a lattice into the flesh, then press the outside of the curved skins to turn these sections inside out, producing easily removable cubes of flesh on the other side. Any flesh still clinging to the stone may be sliced off, or nibbled off as a treat.

Cutting up a Pineapple

Pineapples ripen very rapidly, but will simply not ripen off the tree, so be careful when buying them; they should have a full floral scent and the little leaves at the stalk end should come away easily. Before preparing a pineapple, let it stand upside down for about 30 minutes to let the juices redistribute. Cut off the leafy crown and then cut the fruit across into thick slices. Remove the skin around the edge of the slices and then cut out the woody discs of the core.

Sago and Water Chestnuts with Sweetcorn in Coconut Milk

115 g / 4 oz canned water chestnuts
115 g / 4 oz sago
3 tablespoons sugar
115 g / 4 oz canned sweetcorn
225 ml / 8 fl oz coconut milk
pinch of salt, or more to taste

PREPARATION

Drain the water chestnuts and chop them finely.
Bring a pan of water to the boil and boil the sago in it for
1 minute only. Drain well in a colander and rinse under cold
running water.

COOKING

In a large pan, bring 4 small cups of water to the boil and add the
sugar.
When the sugar has dissolved, add the water chestnuts and
sweetcorn.
Bring back to the boil and add the sago followed by the coconut
milk and salt.
Serve hot.

Water Chestnuts

The Chinese water chestnut is used as both a vegetable and a
fruit. The fibrous brown skin cloaks a nugget of firm white
flesh that has a lovely subtle sweet flavour and a satisfying
crunchy texture. As the skinning is such a chore and canned
water chestnuts keep much of their flavour and most of their
texture, I recommend using the canned variety.

Mango with Cherries

The glorious colours of this simple plate make it a very dramatic-
looking finale to a meal, and the flavour combination is
unbeatable.

2 ripe mangoes
85 g / 3 oz ripe red cherries
1 lemon or lime

PREPARATION

Cut off chunks of mango and prepare as described on page 142,
discarding the stones.
Arrange the chunks on a plate, squeeze over the lemon or lime
juice and scatter the cherries around.

Papaya with Ginger Sauce

1 ripe papaya
5-cm / 2-inch piece of ginger, peeled
2–3 chunks of stem ginger in syrup
3 tablespoons maple syrup

PREPARATION

Cut the papaya lengthwise into four quarters and remove the
seeds.
Carefully slice the papaya flesh away from the skin, keeping the
skin quarters intact. Cut the flesh into pieces and pile them back
into the skin quarters.
Cut the fresh ginger into matchstick shreds.
Slice the stem ginger.

COOKING

Put ½ a small cup of water in a small pan,
add the shredded fresh ginger and
bring to the boil. Stir well until
light brown and remove.
Add the maple syrup and boil
until thick.
Pour over the papaya.
Garnish with the
sliced stem
ginger to
serve.

Appendix

Now you've got your shiny new wok, all the right things in your cupboards and the recipes under your belt, there follows all that you need to complete the Nancy Lam Experience – guidelines on how to make delicious and satisfying meals from my dishes and a few notes on what to drink with my food. There are also some useful addresses of places to find more exotic ingredients. Let your fingers do the wokking!

Nancy's Menu-maker

I know from experience that the worry most Westerners have about Oriental food is how to compose the dishes into whole satisfactory meals (I see that every night in the way people order!). It really is easier than it seems, but to help you there follow a range of sample menus for all occasions – and for different numbers of people – to get you started and give you some ideas.

Obviously you try to get a good balance of types of ingredient (fish, meat, poultry, vegetables), also a good mix of colours and textures (something smooth, something crunchy, etc.). If you can manage, also try for a balance of wet (with lots of gravy or sauce) and dry dishes. The real secret is to make sure there is ENOUGH! If you are in any doubt, just add in an extra rice or noodle dish. It won't cost you much more and if isn't all used up (fat chance!) it can always make lunch the next day!

Romantic Diner à Deux

Lobster Nancy's Style
(page 34)

Beef with Ginger and Brandy
(page 92)

Fried Rice with Nuts
(page 124)

Mango with Cherries
(page 144)

Nancy's Sunday Lunch for 4

Steamed Fish with Ginger and Spring Onion
(page 50)

Sambal Prawns
(page 34)

Stir-fried Asparagus
(page 26)

boiled rice

Banana in Coconut Sauce
(page 140)

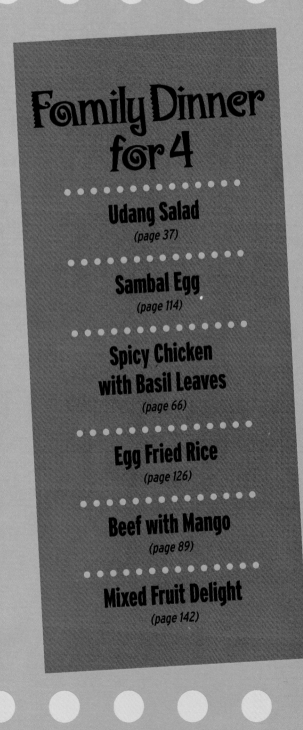

Family Dinner for 4

Udang Salad
(page 37)

Sambal Egg
(page 114)

**Spicy Chicken
with Basil Leaves**
(page 66)

Egg Fried Rice
(page 126)

Beef with Mango
(page 89)

Mixed Fruit Delight
(page 142)

Buffet Party for 12

Udang Salad
(page 37, make double quantity)

Lamb Curry
(page 100)

Curry Puffs
(page 60, make double quantity)

Sesame Chilli Pork
(page 81)

**Savoury Pineapple
and Coriander Salad**
(page 117)

**'Brambly Apples' Stuffed
with Pork and Mushrooms**
(page 78, cut them in quarters)

Rainbow Rice
(page 122)

Bakmie Goreng
(page 130)

Sweet Potato with Ginger
(page 142)

Pancakes Stuffed with Coconut
(page 140)

Vegetarian Lunch for 6

Vegetarian Clay Pot
(page 108)

Deep-fried Aubergine
(page 118)

**Beancurd with Lemon
and Lime Sauce**
(page 110)

Smoky Broccoli with Ginger
(page 107)

Fried Rice with Nuts
(page 124)

Mee Sayur
(page 128)

**Sago and Water Chestnuts
with Sweetcorn in Coconut Milk**
(page 144)

Celebration Meal for 4

Sambal Mussels
(page 26)

Stir-fry Salad
(page 107)

Mushroom Lamb with Chilli
(page 99)

Shocking Chicken Wings
(page 64)

Hokkien Mee
(page 132)

**Pancakes Stuffed
with Coconut**
served with vanilla ice-cream
(page 140)

Budget Meal for 8

Dry Chicken Curry
(page 71)

Party Beef
(page 89)

Stir-fried Beansprouts
(page 104)

boiled rice

Stewed Tofu and Hard-boiled Eggs with Five-spice
(page 108)

Mee Sayur
(page 128)

Banana in Coconut Sauce
(page 140)

Picnic for 6

Curry Puffs
(page 60)

Prawn Toasts
(page 23)

Nancy's Favourite Spare Ribs
(page 84)

Ayam Goreng Jakarta
(page 56)

Savoury Pineapple and Coriander Salad
(page 117)

Beef Fried Rice
(page 125)

Star Fruit with Lime Sauce
(page 138)

Ben's Barbecue Party for 8

Udang Salad
(page 37)

Otar Otar
(page 44)

Shocking Chicken Wings
(page 64)

Chicken Satay
(page 25)

Nancy's Favourite Spare Ribs
(page 84)

Barbecue Beef
(page 92)

Babi Satay
with Pineapple Sauce
(page 78)

Sayur Satay, Kachang Sauce
(page 112)

boiled rice

Mixed Fruit Delight
(page 142)

Fast Meal for 4

Stir-fried Asparagus
(page 26)

Mee Daging
(page 128)

Spicy Chicken
with Basil Leaves
(page 66)

Mixed Fruit Delight
(page 142)

TV Dinner for 2

Easy but Impressive Meal for 6

Posh Dinner Party for 4

Prawn Toasts
(page 23)

Sambal Mussels
(page 26)

Stewed Duck with Five-spice Powder
(page 75)

Smoky Broccoli with Ginger
(page 107)

Rainbow Rice
(page 122)

Mixed Fruit Delight
(page 142)

Cool Meal for a Hot Day for 4

Garlic Prawns in the Shell
(page 38)

Chicken Salad with Five-spice
(page 74)

Savoury Pineapple and Coriander Salad
(page 117)

Nasi Lemak
(page 126)

Star Fruit with Lime Sauce
(page 138)

What to Drink with Nancy's Food

It seems to be modern wisdom that only beer can be drunk with Southeast Asian food because of its up-front and forceful flavours – and believe me lots of beer does get drunk with my food! However, the range of alternatives is much wider than you would think! For example, with the more Chinese dishes, green tea makes a refreshing and appropriate accompaniment.

Dom Perignon '47, shaken and not stirred, of course!

When it comes to wine though, it is obviously just daft to serve a delicate fine wine against chilli-hot and lime-sour food, but if you go for a simple light refreshing white you can get really rewarding results — and such wines tend to be cheaper so you can afford to try a few.

Even if you normally hate them, go for a slightly less than dry wine, say a Riesling, as the hint of sweetness (just a hint, and the wine needs to have a fairly acid undertow) really works with hot and spicy food. Also the widely available and very popular range of Australian Chardonnays has great fruitiness that really works with complex food flavours — provided you avoid anything that has been aged in oak, as that somehow tips the combination into the bitter end of the spectrum.

If you want to go for a red wine, again get something young and fresh (eh, Ben?), like a Beaujolais or a fruity Australian (mmmm, that's for me). And, of course, a good bottle of bubbly will work every time, no matter what the food!

Great combinations:

Rioja (young, unoaked) with fried rice dishes (red or white, according to whether containing meat, poultry or fish).
Bardolino with beef noodle dishes.
Chilled dry **rosé** with Garlic Prawns *(page 38)*.
Californian Zinfandel with barbecued meat.
Lightly chilled young **Beaujolais** with my Stuffed Salmon Rolls *(page 43)*

Index

Nancy's Guide to Shopping

For those who don't have good local shops and supermarkets and so may have difficulty in finding less common ingredients, the following may be of some help:

Amaranth *(mostly Thai ingredients)*
345 Garratt Lane, London SW18
0181 871 3466

Bhavins Foods *(general Oriental foods)*
193-197 Upper Tooting Road, London SW17
0181 672 7531

Candycraig Mushrooms *(mail order mushrooms and Oriental vegetables)*
Cairnquheen Cottage, Crathie, Ballater AB35 5TD
01339 742342

Deepak Foods *(general Oriental foods)*
953-959 Garratt Lane, London SW17
0181 767 7810

Greencades *(mail-order herbs and spices)*
No 5, The Apprentice Shop Building
Merton Abbey Mills Craft Village, Watermill Way,
South Wimbledon, London SW19 2RD
0181 543 0519

Hoo Hing Oriental Food Specialists *(general, also branches in Mitcham, Surrey, and London NW10)*
Hoo Hing House,
Eastway Commercial Centre, London E9 5NR
0181 533 2811

Jekka's Herb Farm *(mail order herbs and Oriental vegetables)*
Rose Cottage, Shellards Lane,
Alveston, Bristol, Avon BS12 2SY
01454 418878

New England Lobsters International Ltd *(live lobsters, shellfish and prawns)*
Smuggler's House, 17 Lydden Road, London SW18 4LT
0181 877 1175

Sri Thai *(mostly Thai ingredients, with a little Chinese, including a wide range of fresh fruit, herbs and vegetables)*
Oriental Food Centre, 56 Shepherds Bush Road, London W6 7LT
0171 602 0621

Wing Yip *(general, also branches in Cricklewood and Manchester)*
544 Purley Way, Croydon CR0 4RF
0181 688 4880

Acknowledgements

The author and publishers would like to thank the following for their help in putting together this book:

Dennis Edwards at John Austin & Co. Ltd, Wholesale Florists, New Covent Garden, London
ICTC, Norwich *(tableware)*
Joseph Chua Seng Guan, Sarawak, East Malaysia *(tableware)*
Evans Gray & Hood Foods, London
Evergreen Exterior Services, Plant & Shrub Wholesalers, Croydon
International Cooking and Tableware Co. Ltd, Norwich
Natural Wood Flooring Co. Ltd., London SW18
Stannard Butchers, Tooting, London
Wing Yip, Croydon

Nancy would also like to express her heartfelt thanks to:
Lewis Esson for all his inspiration, patience and hard work on the text;
John Lawrence Jones and his assistant Steve Aland for their creativity and the beautiful pictures of the food (and her);
John Millar for his atmospheric black-and-whites;
Nigel Soper for the glorious and exciting design job;
Sarah, Christopher and everyone else at Fourth Estate;
and last, but by no means least, her husband Ben for all his support and her lovely daughters – Yang Mei for all her typing and general help, and Yangtze for using her great skills to make her look so good.
Finally, Nancy thanks the Lord for having given her the opportunity and strength to do all this.